"For any pastor desiring to make an impact in the business world, Shepherding Horses (Volume II) is a must-read. Humphreys offers solid guidelines for anyone wishing to develop a spiritual legacy in the workplace."

BOB RECCORD
Founder, Total Life Impact, Inc.

"Kent Humphreys is one of the few people I know who could write this book. He has lived out his passion to follow Christ in the marketplace and has communicated this vision to hundreds of current and would-be pastors. If enough pastors and businesspersons will follow the model of Jesus as set forth here it could revolutionize both their churches and their vocational worlds! This is a must-read for all those committed to empowering lay persons in the 'second reformation'!"

LEIGHTON FORD
President, Leighton Ford Ministries, Charlotte, North Carolina

"Shepherding Horses (Volume II) is a superb guide for ministers who desire to see their lay people in the marketplace make an impact for Christ. Kent Humphreys is uniquely qualified to provide these insights based on his faithfulness to the local church and his remarkable success in bringing Christ to the marketplace."

PAIGE PATTERSON
President, Southwestern Baptist Theological Seminary

"No one is more overlooked and underchallenged in the church today than the gifted business leader. Kent Humphreys shows how pastors and business leaders can work together to reach the marketplace and build the church...and enjoy the process. This is a must-read!"

ROC BOTTOMLY
Pastor, Our Lord's Community, Oklahoma City, Oklahoma

"Shepherding Horses (Volume II) is a red-alert wakeup call for the 90 percent of American pastors not yet tuned in to what the Holy Spirit is currently doing among workplace believers. In it, Kent Humphreys has built solid bridges that every church leader urgently needs to cross."

C. PETER WAGNER
Chancellor, Wagner Leadership Institute

kent humphreys

SHEPHERDING
HORSES

~ VOLUME II ~

a PASTOR'S GUIDE *to*
EQUIPPING WORKPLACE LEADERS

Cover design: C R Design, Charles Rogez
Creative team: Nanci McAlister, Greg Clouse, Cara Iverson, Kathy Mosier, Glynese Northam

Some of the anecdotal illustrations in this book are true to life and are included with the permission of the persons involved. All other illustrations are composites of real situations, and any resemblance to people living or dead is coincidental.

Humphreys, Kent.
  Shepherding Horses -Volume II: A Pastor's Guide for Equipping Workplace Leaders
Includes bibliographical references.
  ISBN 1-57683-355-0
  1. Evangelistic work. 2. Witness bearing (Christianity) 3.Work--Religious aspects--Christianity. I. Title.

To Jack and Bonnie Humphreys

My parents were the first to show me what a difference

Jesus Christ can make in a life. They have continually modeled

to me what a leader is and what a leader does.

CONTENTS

Note from Author   9

Foreword   13

Acknowledgments   15

Introduction   19

    I. ESTABLISHING ENCOURAGING RELATIONSHIPS   25

II.THE FORMAT OF THE MINISTRY   41

    III. THE PASTOR AS EQUIPPER   63

    IV. OVERCOMING OBSTACLES TO WORKPLACE MINISTRY 81

    V. KEY MENTORING AREAS   99

    VI. CREATIVE APPROACHES TO MINISTRY IN THE MARKETPLACE 113

    VII. MODELING THE MESSAGE IN A SECULAR CULTURE 129

    VIII. THE CHALLENGE TO REPRODUCE   141

    IX. TWO WARNINGS   157

    X. LEAVING A LEGACY   169

Conclusion   177

Appendix I: Sample Meeting Topics   179

Appendix II: Resources   187

Appendix III: Resources   189

Notes   198

About the Author   200

NOTE FROM THE AUTHOR

Shepherding Horses, A Pastor's Guide for Equipping Workplace Leaders, Implementing the Plan was first published in 2004 under the title of Lasting Investments. My original manuscript was titled Shepherding Horses and that was the title of the first chapter in the package that I presented to several major Christian publishers in 2002. I used the analogy of horses and sheep. Pastors get training in seminary on how to take care of the sheep, but they get little help on how to deal with aggressive workplace leaders (the wild horses!). The publisher that gave us a contract thought that the analogy was a little too much for their conservative audience, so the chapter was taken out, the book title was changed, and Lasting Investments was published in 2004.

I continued to love the analogy of shepherds, horses, and sheep to pastors, workplace leaders, and congregations, and shared it as a message at conferences of key church and marketplace leaders. Audiences responded in such a positive way to it. They loved the analogy, too. In the fall of 2006, I was speaking in Singapore to a large pastors' conference with 700 leaders from seventeen different nations. I spoke four times, and the audience responded overwhelmingly because they identified so strongly. (They even began adding their own analogies about chickens, donkeys, and mules!) I thought that if this message was so well received and understood by leaders who were hearing it in their second language half way around the world, then it should be well received in my own nation. I returned home to tell Davidene that we had to put those messages into a small book as soon as possible. So, we published "Shepherding Horses" and presented it at a large U.S. workplace conference the following January. It received the same tremendous response. One lady was crying, telling me that she finally understood herself for the first time. Everywhere that I went the "horses" analogy followed me.

Over the last few years Shepherding Horses has been translated into nine or ten languages and been printed and distributed in Europe, Asia, Latin American, Africa, and other places. So, even though Shepherding Horses was published after the original book, it is really an introduction to this book. It shows the need for relationships between pastors and workplace leaders. Many relationships have now been built between leaders in nations around the world, because we have started to talk about the elephant in the room that had not been discussed previously. Pastors now attend our workplace events and business leaders are working with pastors to see real transformation in their cities.

The book that you now hold in your hands has been updated with the latest resources and web sites to support the changes from the last couple of years in the expanding global workplace movement. It is the implementation plan that can be used by any pastor or workplace leader to equip leaders in the church and release them into the workplaces of the city. This step by step process has been proven over and over. True transformation does not happen in events or large groups, but it occurs through one on one or small group relationships. I hope that you will find this to be a very helpful guide.

Although this book stands alone, it is even more helpful if both the pastor and workplace leader first read and discuss Shepherding Horses together. Then, they should use this guide, Shepherding Horses: Implementing the Plan, to start the small group process. Used together, the introductory book and this guide will give you a good start on equipping your workplace leaders for Christ. We stand ready to help you in any way that we can. May the Holy Spirit give you courage and creativity as you seek to serve Him in this way.

FOREWORD

⁓

IN *SHEPHERDING HORSES (VOLUME II): A Pastor's Guide to Equipping Workplace Leaders,* Kent Humphreys draws from years of experience as he writes about the passion of his heart, counseling business leaders and pastors. This is a most practical resource for pastors developing ministry outside the four walls of their churches.

Someone recently said that the "First" Reformation took the Word of God to the common man and woman; the "Second" Reformation is taking the *work* of God to the common man and woman. That time is now. The greatest potential ministry in the world today is the marketplace. Christ's greatest labor force is those men and women already in that environment.

Several years ago, I was teaching witnessing classes in preparation for a Billy Graham crusade. After the class, a woman mentioned to me that she was a missionary. "Where do you work?" I asked. She said that she worked for a major accounting firm. I was confused; I did not know of any national accounting firm that had missionaries or chaplains. "What do you do there?" I inquired. "I'm a Certified Public Accountant," she replied. Intrigued, I asked, "How do you do both at the same place?" "I'm a missionary cleverly disguised as an accountant," she answered.

That is what our world needs. Our pastors cannot go daily into the marketplace. Our nation is becoming more and more secular, lacking a church background and enough of a comfort level to even visit a local church. So, the greatest legacy pastors can leave is to train workplace leaders in their churches to minister in their own workplaces to ensure that every mission field represented by every church receives proper ministry.

A pastor can see a great harvest come back into the church as these workplace leaders share Christ with their colleagues, begin to disciple them, and eventually bring them into the fellowship of the church.

Too often when the church has a "Ministry Sunday" to recruit workers, the pastor lists only those areas within the *church building* that need volunteers. An outstanding high school teacher will feel called to the teaching ministry of the church youth, which is quite good. However, how many churches anoint and pray for that high school teacher as he or she works in the difficult mission field of the local high school, potentially touching hundreds of souls for Christ every day?

If pastors follow Kent Humphreys' step-by-step process, they will not only see the ministry of the church flourish, but will also see an incredible impact on the people of the church who are sovereignly and providentially placed to be missionaries cleverly disguised as accountants, secretaries, CEOs, and maintenance workers. No concerned individual Christian inside the church should be without training to accomplish this as a personal ministry.

I watch with anticipation to see how God will use this book and its principles as expressed through Kent Humphreys' life, teachings, and writings.

TOM PHILLIPS, *Vice President of Training*
Billy Graham Evangelistic Association

ACKNOWLEDGMENTS

MY WIFE, DAVIDENE, has been my constant encourager, advisor, editor, and partner in this project. Without her sacrificial work, writing skills, and sage wisdom, this book never would have been completed. She has continually urged me to write about my passion and given me the courage to attempt this manuscript. God has gifted her with the ability to help me and many others pursue their dreams.

This work would not have been possible without the participation of the pastors and lay leaders who have painstakingly completed our surveys. I would not have undertaken this project without the encouragement of friends and pastors. My own pastor, Ray Ivey, has constantly supported my efforts to actively minister in the marketplace.

The tireless typing of my assistant, Cathy Burris, makes these words legible. The editorial assistance of Patricia Farewell has been invaluable. Thank you, Nanci McAlister, for being the champion of our cause. Thank you, Greg Clouse, for your patience and helpfulness. You gave structure and style to the ideas of a business entrepreneur.

Finally, without the mentoring and example of Gene Warr, Ford Madison, Pete Hammond, and countless others, I would have never been able to channel the passion that I have for reaching the workplace. I humbly acknowledge that I am just a businessman who has been touched by Christ and impacted by hundreds of other fellow marketplace believers in the daily challenges of the business world.

"AS YOU SENT ME INTO THE WORLD, I HAVE SENT THEM INTO THE WORLD. . . .

MY PRAYER

IS NOT FOR THEM ALONE. I PRAY ALSO FOR THOSE WHO WILL BELIEVE IN ME THROUGH THEIR MESSAGE, THAT ALL OF THEM

MAY BE ONE, FATHER, JUST AS YOU ARE IN ME AND I

AM IN YOU.

MAY THEY ALSO BE IN US SO THAT THE WORLD MAY BELIEVE THAT YOU HAVE SENT ME."

—JOHN 17:18,20-21

INTRODUCTION

JESUS CHRIST'S HEARTFELT prayer for His closest friends, His disciples, was for relationships, rare and deep — intimate unity only possible when created by God the Father through His Son. Such relationships result in change — in a life and in the world. He modeled to us that these bonds are the keys in ministering to others and in training those who would carry on the work of the gospel.

I have spent thirty years in the marketplace ministering as a business owner. My desire is to assist pastors in deepening their relationships with the workplace leaders in their churches and maximizing their ministries through them. I want to encourage pastors and help them to better understand, equip, and release their workplace leaders in order that these men and women may become more effective in the kingdom ministries into which God has called them *and* in the churches into which God has placed them.

God has given me a heart for pastors such as you. Years ago I began to notice that pastors and I would relate easily when I met them while speaking at conferences, seminars, and local churches. They would openly share their hearts with me because I was neither in their organization nor one of their church laity. Several of

these relationships have developed into deep, long-term friendships. Since then, other pastors have sought me out in order to
understand their lay leaders. In turn, I have sought out pastors in
our city to find out how I could pray for them, encourage them,
and assist them in relating to leaders such as myself. My own pastor
and I have become trusted friends, and he is an encourager for me
as I have endeavored to minister to business associates, pastors,
and leaders in the workplace.

As many of these friendships developed, I began to realize that
you, as a pastor, face many of the same difficulties, challenges, and
times of loneliness that I face as an executive. I do not claim to understand completely the daily pressures that you encounter; however, I
believe I have endured many similar pressures as a CEO and business
owner. I also found that even though they desire it, few of my workplace friends have developed deep relationships with their pastors.

When both my son and son-in-law became pastors, I became
even more convinced that God was calling me to help build bridges
between pastors and leaders in the marketplace. I have done exten-
sive research with pastors from twenty states. In addition, I have
surveyed and personally interviewed hundreds of marketplace leaders and clergy in numerous churches.

By the way, I define a workplace leader as anyone who leads or
influences others in the workplace, even if he or she does not have
a specific position of authority. Anyone who people follow is a
leader, who, under Christ's control, has the opportunity to impact
countless others for Him in the daily work environment.

In the pages that follow, I will freely use God's Word, specifically the book of Mark and the model of Jesus, as a pattern for ministry. This book is not a study of Mark, but rather a study of how Jesus related to the workplace leaders whom He encountered and how He equipped His disciples for ministry in the world.

The purpose of this book is both theoretical and practical. The goal is to choose a small group of men and women in your church who are leaders in the community and in their workplace. They will form the nucleus of a new ministry, just as the disciples did for Jesus. I will outline how to initially approach each of them, explain how to form the group and get started, and even provide some topic ideas for your meetings together. You will become mentor and trainer as these folks learn from the Word, support each other, and strategize and problem-solve about individual ministries in the workplace. Eventually, you will release this group so that these leaders can reproduce themselves while you begin a new group.

If you choose to adopt this plan, the scope of your church's evangelism, outreach, and discipleship can significantly expand. You likely will find that key leaders have *more* time to spend meeting the volunteer needs of your church and that their involvement has a freer and more fulfilled quality. And I believe that you personally will sense more fulfillment and spiritual energy than you have felt in years — by focusing not on organization, budgets, buildings, or programs but solely on your relationships with the leaders in your church and the resulting impact on a secular community.

Implementing this ministry into your schedule may sound daunting, because time is your most precious and rare commodity. But if you will allow yourself to seriously consider and pray about this, I think you will find that the idea is time-efficient and concise, exceedingly doable, and ultimately rewarding.

You might also think about giving this book to a pastor friend in your town who would consider starting this ministry in his church. You could talk and plan together, implement the steps at the same time, and encourage each other along the way. It is always easier to begin something new with a friend for support.

Whether you do this with a friend or not, the exciting thing is releasing leaders to use their platforms and gifts. You will have developed men and women who are equipped to "do the work of the ministry" in their own spheres of influence and are reproducers as well. It is what Jesus did, what He modeled for us to do, and what He will empower you to do.

THEREFORE,
SINCE THROUGH
GOD'S
MERCY

WE HAVE THIS
M I N I S T R Y,
WE DO NOT
LOSE
H E A R T.

—2 CORINTHIANS 4:1

CHAPTER I

ESTABLISHING ENCOURAGING RELATIONSHIPS

PASTOR GREG WALTERS sat at his desk, staring at the opposite wall; it had been a long day. The daughter of one church family had just lost a five-year battle with leukemia, and her funeral had taken place this morning. Although the day itself was sunshiny glorious — the cemetery decorated with autumn's crown of red and gold — and the church had turned out en masse to comfort and support the girl's parents, these things were always hard. Greg felt drained, knowing that he, too, would miss the giggly ten-year-old.

Greg had taken some time after lunch to think, read his Bible, and pray. Extra time with the Lord always renewed his peace, strength, and positive attitude. This afternoon he had counseled a couple preparing for their marriage (a happy hour), followed by a counseling session with a young man battling anorexia (a sober and troubling one). Starting to feel weary, Greg looked forward to the Wednesday evening church dinner, Bible study, and prayer time. After that, he would be presenting several new ideas to the Personnel Committee.

It was now 10 P.M., and Greg should be home. Instead he sat in his office, feeling a mixture of agitation and concern. Robert Miller had not been at the Personnel Committee meeting, calling Greg at the last minute to apologize that he had to work late. Could he catch up with Pastor Walters over lunch in a few days to discuss the new issues? Of course, Greg had said yes, but he was more frustrated than he had let on. Robert had no way of knowing how excited Greg had been to present his new ideas and how ineffective the meeting had been without Robert present, but the problem went beyond that.

Greg worried about Robert's focus on work. Could it be that his focus to make money was growing stronger than his focus to love God and his church? Robert's desire to be included and to participate in the church's programs *seemed* to be as strong as ever, and his wife and kids still came to everything, but more and more often Robert seemed preoccupied with work, and he had recently missed several events such as tonight's meeting. Maybe Robert's promotion to CEO had gone to his head.

Greg had thought about this dilemma before — so much so that he had asked Cheryl, another minister on the church staff, if she had sensed anything wrong with Debbie, Robert's wife. She had not noticed anything different about Debbie's demeanor but would make it a point to listen more carefully at the weekly women's Bible study. Cheryl did mention that during a recent conversation about how hard it was to get the kids to church when Robert was out of town, Debbie had seemed to take it in stride, expressing gratitude, in fact, that Robert was situated where "God wanted him."

Cheryl had gone on to say that she *had* noticed a similar pattern with Susan Voight, who had bought a boutique a year ago. Susan had been so excited about it but was now having trouble keeping up with all of her obligations in the church's women's ministry. To make matters worse, Tracy Barrington had recently gone to work for Susan, and Cheryl was concerned that she, too, would experience the pull of two worlds. Greg wondered whether it would always be this way with business-oriented people. Could they not be leaders at work and in church at the same time? It was a confusing situation, at best, and would take more thought and prayer.

At 10 P.M. that same evening, in an office across town, Robert Miller sat at his desk, staring at the wall opposite him. What a day! He had been elated when his promotion to CEO had materialized, because he had long felt a need to find ways to show Christ's love to the people he was around every day. Now he had the authority to make things happen for good for his employees as well as their families. He felt tremendous responsibility for them and had been praying that God would give him direction. He wanted the company atmosphere to be that of an extended family, and he was trying to be sensitive to people's needs. He hadn't expected what happened next. As folks became convinced that he really did care about them, they began to let him see some of their personal battles. Just before closing time today, Jim, the man whose office was next to Robert's, poked his head in the door.

"Can I talk to you for a minute?"

"Sure, come on in."

After excusing himself for a minute to call the church and let the pastor know that he wouldn't be there for a Personnel Committee meeting, the two men settled down to talk. Robert worried about missing the meeting because he knew that new business would be presented, but he would call Pastor Walters tomorrow to explain. Guilt gnawed at the edges of his thoughts.

Jim's benign comments initiated two hours of revelation of heart-wrenching fear and worry; Jim suspected that his son might be an alcoholic and that his daughter was probably sexually active with a boy whom he loathed and distrusted. This man had been trying to run the operations of a multimillion-dollar firm today while his mind was waging war for his kids. Robert listened, talked a little, and prayed with Jim, who seemed to be more settled when he left. It was obvious to Robert that he needed to find more help for Jim, someone he could talk to regularly and who knew more than Robert did in these areas. Where would he find such help?

He needed to find help for Mark and his family, too. Mark, who lived in another state, was a salesperson for the company. He had an important territory, and the work could not be entrusted to better hands. Mark was a hardworking man of integrity and honor. But this morning he had found out that his cancer, which he had thought was detected early and could be easily treated, had actually metastasized throughout his body. Mark had very little time. His family was devastated. Robert had to act fast to help this family and to help the company. If a family ever needed to know Jesus, it was Mark's family — now. Robert realized that this was a huge opportunity to share God's love with them, and he would. He would also look into the health insurance issue tomorrow. How could they take care of Mark's widow? What kind of care did Mark need now? Who could he send to handle Mark's territory?

Then there was the matter that had been brought to him by the warehouse manager. The company had recently hired a number of people, many of whom did not speak English. They were good workers, and fortunately enough of them could communicate with the manager and each other to provide efficiency. Yesterday, one of them had asked the manager if he knew of a minister who could perform a wedding; they were new to the area and did not have a church. They also hoped the minister could visit a family member in the hospital. It seems the mother had difficulty with a home birth, and both she and her baby had to be rushed to the hospital and admitted. The extended family was frantic due to a lack of understanding about what had happened and how the hospital system worked. Robert knew that something must be done for them, possibly for the whole community. He could visit the family with an interpreter, but the help must go beyond that. Maybe having a chaplain who came regularly to the company would be a start. He would look into that and other solutions, too. He needed time to think and pray.

Robert was overwhelmed with excitement that his prayer to be able to influence people around him for God was being answered, but he was also anxious about what to do next with all of these opportunities. He wished he had someone to talk to about it. The logical person would be Pastor Walters, but Robert had ambivalent feelings right now about the church. He suspected his only use there was to provide money and a presence in committee meetings. He felt no one understood the dilemmas he faced, and he fought guilt over lacking time to be more involved. It seemed right that the church should be the place to turn to for ideas regarding ministering for the Lord, but Robert could think of no programs or classes there that would remotely address those issues.

———

These hypothetical scenarios are repeated over and over in real churches and businesses. It is a tragedy that people such as these, who have so much in common, rarely cross paths except to greet each other in a hallway at church or to briefly chat about surface interests. What would it look like if they were to join their considerable forces to minister to the workplace while strengthening the effect of the church in the community?

THE DILEMMA

Let's begin by looking at the common issues that both you, as a pastor, and the workplace leader face. Both leaders are in upper management of their respective organizations, and both can feel "alone at the top," isolated. They feel the pressure of being responsible for many people who look to them for vision and wisdom. They both need encouragement but find few, if any, people with whom they can communicate honestly. They both work hard with great intentions but often find their motivations misunderstood.

So the question that continues to pull at my heart is this: If we (pastors and workplace leaders) have so much in common, why haven't we tried to understand each other and work together? Although many reasons contribute to the common gap in relationships between pastors and business leaders, a few stood out in the results of our surveys. First, there is the phenomenon I call the *intimidation factor*. Many people who are influential in their businesses feel intimidated by the spiritual life of their pastor. It is a puzzle: In the business world they can hold their own, but when comparing themselves to their pastor on the platform every Sunday morning, they think they could never match up. And so they run back to their comfortable working world. Conversely, pastors can be intimidated by workplace leaders, especially the high-powered executive types. There is a fear of the control that they can exert by use of their personalities or their money.

Second is the *vulnerability factor*. The simple fact is that deeper relationships require a certain level of openness. Most people fear vulnerability, and men have a harder time with it than do women. One pastor put it this way: "I find it difficult to talk about my own insecurities and feelings of inadequacy, and I have achieved this level of vulnerability with maybe four men in the church at different times. It is risky." That pastor is correct; it is risky. After all, if I reveal my open and honest self to another, what will the other do with the information? Will I be rejected or misunderstood? Will the information inappropriately be shared with another? We must come to realize that such relationships are worth the risk.

Even Jesus sought the intimacy and encouragement of sharing His most important moments with a trusted few. Although Jesus had a huge congregation, only Peter, James, and John were invited to share the Mount of Transfiguration experience or the prayer time in the Garden of Gethsemane. Jesus had the most critical mission and carried the greatest burden of responsibility in history. He experienced time pressure and was inundated with crises to solve, yet He made a point to develop a few trusted relationships with whom to share not just His ministry but also His life. We need the same. It is a fact that the lay leaders in your church could be your greatest encouragers, and you could be the spiritual support system that they need as they learn to minister in their workplaces. I believe that God has something to say to us.

THE SOLUTION

What would happen if you were to choose a few workplace leaders from within your own church and meet with them regularly? The goal of such a small-group meeting would be to help these leaders figure out how to have an effective ministry in their own spheres of influence, while mentoring and encouraging them spiritually along the way. These meetings would involve both praying and looking in the Bible for answers, but most of the ideas for marketplace ministry would come from the brainstorming of the leaders themselves. The leaders will be the greatest resource you have, although there are various other resources available to help accomplish your goals. (We will acquaint you with these later in the book.)

Here is the basic plan, which I will flesh out in subsequent chapters. First, you, as the pastor, pray about which leaders — starting with just a few — to invite into your initial group. Then, meet with each one individually *on their turf.* For example, meet one at the office for a brief tour and then take him or her out to lunch. Present your invitation and ask that leader to pray about joining you and a few other leaders for this experimental group. Set the date for the initial meeting approximately three weeks in advance so that the participants can clear their calendars and you can make these lunch dates without haste.

Meet during lunch or breakfast time, weekly or biweekly, somewhere out in the marketplace. It usually works well to have lunch at the office of one leader, having sandwiches or pizza brought in to conserve time. The meetings start out with folks sharing ministry ideas and basic biblical principles; then, as time progresses, these people become vitally important to each other. They merge into a support group like none of them has ever had before. The leaders learn how to support and encourage you as their pastor, just as you are learning how to help them. The results are exciting.

In *Today God Is First,* a series of marketplace meditations, Os Hillman quotes a Third World pastor:

> We've spent too much time equipping our business people to do our ministries rather than equipping them to do the ministry God has called them to in the first place.... The workplace is the greatest mission field of our day, and yet we do not train business people how to effectively integrate faith into their workplace.... God is removing the wall of separation by speaking to pastors and business people all over the world.[1]

Like Jesus in the first century, this Third World pastor understands that the greatest ministry opportunity today may be through work-place leaders.

Recently, I received an e-mail from Ron Elliott, a Midwestern pastor, who told the following story:

> I visited with one of my laymen [Doug] last night. He has a heart for the Lord and is very gifted in evangelism. He is a taxicab driver and probably works seventy hours a week. He shared with me how he has the opportunity to share with many people each day about Christ. He has more opportunities to share Christ in a week than I have in a year.
>
> He has a Bible study with about ten to fifteen cab drivers on Thursday evenings in the basement of the Omaha public library. (The owner of the cab company is not a Christian and didn't want them to have the Bible study in the company building.) Doug's manager is a Christian and participates in the study. Doug is beginning to develop a vision of reaching cab drivers for Christ. This is an interesting and innovative ministry I never would have thought about. I had Doug share in church last night what God is doing in his life.
>
> Over a year ago he asked the church to pray for a cab driver who was addicted to gambling. That cab driver approached Doug two weeks ago and said, "I am ready." Doug said, "Ready for what?" He said, "I

am ready for God." Doug had the opportunity to lead him to the Lord.

This is what excites me as a pastor – seeing my flock going out during the week where they live and work and impacting their sphere of influence for Christ.

This is what it is all about. Doug has a strong and clear vision of what his ministry should be. Because he has a plan and is time-efficient, he also has time to heavily support Pastor Elliott and his church. It is a win-win situation for both men. Not only do they have a mutual need for each other, but they are also enjoying the mutual benefits of having a close relationship.

— Q & A —

Is this whole idea becoming more intriguing to you? I would like to finish this chapter with several questions that various pastors have asked.

Q: *Why do I need to be the one to initiate this?*
A: Jesus' example to us was such. When He wanted to impart His ministry to people, He could have gone to church leaders. We know from history that at least a few such leaders were open to Him, Nicodemus being one of them. But Jesus chose leaders from the marketplace. Some were already acknowledged public leaders, such as Matthew, and some were leaders only in their own small realm,

such as Peter. Jesus went to each of them on their own turf and invited them to join Him. Then He spoke to them in terms that they understood while they learned to understand spiritual terms. (With Peter, for example, he used fishing terms.) He trained them in their world until they were ready to train others and carry on the mission.

Q: *What advantage would there be for the church if I do this?*

A: First, the church's ministry expands when marketplace leaders are set loose to impact their worlds for Christ. It gives a boost to the ultimate fulfillment of God's Great Commission to us.

Next, the church gains leaders who are more productive and less crisis-driven. They have a plan, and so their decisions are no longer driven by the tyranny of the urgent because they now have a way in place to deal with it.

Finally, the flourishing of outreach ideas will impact others not involved directly with the small group, and the church's outreach will grow.

Q: *What advantage is there to me?*

A: As a pastor, you gain loyal and supportive friends who truly do understand you. A few of them will become your closest confidants. You need them as much as they need you! You also gain focused volunteers for your church programs and for the community in general, not fragmented souls who have good intentions but cannot pull life together into an organized whole.

Q: *Would business leaders really go for this idea?*

A: Yes, they would and they have. The fact is that many business-people have tried to accomplish this for themselves, meeting weekly in the marketplace to brainstorm and encourage each other, because they have not been offered such help by their churches or their pastors.

Q: *What sacrifices would I have to make in order to accomplish this? After all, life is already too busy.*
A: There is a time sacrifice. Something else may have to be limited or omitted from your schedule in order to do it. Initially, there is thinking, praying, and planning time. Then there is an hour for each individual you invite. After that, there is an hour every week or so (depending on how you plan it) for regular meetings. Otherwise, the time demand is flexible, depending on your desired involvement with the individuals or their ministries. There is always an emotional cost of being involved with people, but in this case, the primary emotion is excitement rather than discouragement.

Q: *Exactly how could time be carved out for such a task?*
A: The best times for meetings of this nature are lunch hours and early mornings because people frequently have those times free. It does not add an extra hour during already busy evenings and weekends.

Q: *Can you train men and women together?*
A: Yes, you can. There are distinct advantages to having both sexes involved in your groups. Women have an easier time being open with their feelings and ideas. Their intuition is a God-given ability

that men typically don't possess, so they add important input. On the other hand, men often can see the big picture and the possible pitfalls of ideas more easily than women can. We need each other. It also makes no difference whether the pastor involved is a man or woman. Many churches have both male and female ministers on their staffs, and they can work together with this idea as well. I realize that in the present workplace environment, men-only and women-only groups are the most popular because both genders tend to be more open with same-sex peers, but try to keep your mind open to various possibilities that God may want you to try.

In concluding this chapter, I'd like to share with you my life verse, Philemon 1:7: "For I have come to have much joy and comfort in your love, because the hearts of the saints have been refreshed through you, brother" (NASB). Wherever God has placed me, I have sought to encourage those around me. As we fellowship around the person of Jesus Christ and His Holy Word, may we be encouraged together.

As workplace leaders and pastors, we all have a tendency to be loners and to not open ourselves to intimate relationships with others, particularly those in our own organizations. May God allow us to find each other and to renew and deepen relationships, thus building a foundation for true spiritual fellowship and equipping.

ACTION STEPS

1. Begin by targeting individuals in your church who are leaders in the marketplace or in your community. They may or may not hold positions of leadership in your church. Spend time with God, asking Him to give you these names.

2. Quietly and informally start relationships with these individuals apart from any church program. Plan to spend a morning a week having breakfast with one or two of them together. Spend this time simply getting to know them better. Set a luncheon date and go by their offices and tour their workplaces. They will expect you to have an agenda such as fund-raising or the start of a new program. Your actions will mystify them.

3. Drop them a personal note or card encouraging them about what God is doing in their lives, stating that you are praying for them or thanking them for their friendship.

You might put this book down for a couple of weeks while you think about all of this. You may want to give a copy of the book to a pastor friend with whom you would like to do this project. Take your time. What you are doing is important.

JESUS WENT
UP ON A MOUNTAINSIDE
AND CALLED TO HIM
THOSE HE
WANTED,
AND THEY CAME TO HIM.

HE APPOINTED TWELVE-
DESIGNATING
THEM APOSTLES—THAT
THEY MIGHT BE WITH HIM AND THAT HE MIGHT
SEND THEM OUT
TO PREACH.

—MARK 3:13-14

CHAPTER II

THE FORMAT OF THE MINISTRY

CONSIDER WITH ME one of the most important nights in the life of Jesus. This is probably a familiar passage to you, one on which you may have preached many times. However, this time I want you to see it from the viewpoint of the disciples. In Mark 3, we see Jesus surrounded by the multitudes (see verses 7, 9, 20, and 32). But in verse 13, Jesus slipped away from the crowds and went up on the mountain. (The corresponding passage in Luke 6:12 tells us that He spent the entire night in prayer.) We are told that when the morning came, He chose the Twelve. Jesus appointed the Twelve for two purposes: first, so that they would be with Him; and second, so that He could send them out.

Your most important job as a pastor is to do these two things. You must spend time with your leaders and send them out. Let us look at why Jesus chose to make the focus of His ministry on this small group.

Preaching and teaching occur in large groups, but normally interaction and change take place in small groups (an average small group being defined as six to twelve people). Jesus modeled the Twelve to us because that is what works. An increasing number of churches today are built around the concept of cell groups, house churches, accountability groups, small home Bible studies, prayer groups, or fellowship groups. You have less control of the agenda but far greater participation in a small group than when you preach. In the more intimate setting, members can be vulnerable, share real life problems, and examine the Word together.

THE PURPOSE OF THE GROUP

A group ministry to leaders could be the most productive one of your life, for you as well as for them. Leaders in the workplace need to become sensitive to you as their pastor. They need to see you as a real person with the same needs that they have. As you spend time with them as Jesus did, they will begin to understand you and realize that you are just like them but with a different position. When church members put you on a pedestal and expect you to do all of their "religious" work, it is harmful to both sides.

Workplace leaders must establish new relationships with you while realizing that God has ordained you to help equip them to do the work of the ministry. I can tell you that your greatest need is probably encouragement. The lay leaders in your church also need the same encouragement, but more than that, they need the affirmation that they are ministers for Christ. They really want some hands-on coaching to help them integrate the spiritual and the secular, their faith and their work. Only as you understand this will you be able to relate to and equip them.

Both you and your workplace leaders need to look carefully at

God's Word to be reminded of some basic principles. We all tend to get so busy building religious institutions and profitable businesses that we forget God's objective: to bring the people in the lost world to Jesus. Workplace leaders are daily seeking to make a profit while you, as a pastor, are continually pursuing the demanding task of leading a group of volunteers. Each of you struggles to survive. God wants you to join together to make a difference for eternity. You must concentrate, not on your differences, but on your similarities and begin the journey of serving Christ together as a team!

However, let me caution you: You and your leaders must be patient enough to wait for the results of your efforts; sometimes it takes years. There is the possibility that this ministry could be extremely productive, but many of the results could be located in other parts of your city, your state, and even the nation. This ministry to leaders will require no additional staff, no budget, and no buildings.

This ministry to workplace leaders is biblical and simple, but it is not institutional. It does not tend to automatically build membership, buildings, budgets, or reputations. It does, however, build the body of Christ, both numerically and in maturity. It allows members to use their gifts and callings in their spheres of influence to passionately proclaim Jesus Christ. This small-group ministry to leaders will dramatically increase the number of people that your church has involved in personal ministry and will broaden the scope of your church's influence. Will you actively endorse this knowing that God is in it and will richly bless it?

HOW TO CHOOSE MEMBERS
FOR YOUR GROUP

Here is how you get started. Remember, the key is relationships, not methods. Jesus wanted the Twelve to be *with* Him. Of course, He had ministry goals, but He also desired fellowship for its own sake.

You have already begun asking God to give you six to twelve workplace leaders in your church. Look for people with a good heart and those that have influence at work and in the community. They may not necessarily have leadership positions in your church. Look for leaders who are busy in their work, who are "change agents" not really satisfied with the status quo. These may be leaders who are not at the church every time the doors are opened, but nonetheless have a life focused on God and other people. You may want to have a group consisting of both men and women leaders, or you may choose to have a group just for women or one just for men.

Even if you have had several months to build relationships, it will take several weeks or even months to get your group together. Do not move too quickly or get ahead of God's direction. If this is the beginning of September, for instance, you might plan for a start date of the first week in January. If you did not pause after chapter 1, why not stop right now and spend a few days praying over a list of names?

When Jesus chose His twelve disciples, He used a definite method. Among other things, He chose a group of people with a variety of occupations and personalities. If we were to look at them and determine who their counterparts might be in the twenty-first century, the list might look something like this:

* Peter, Andrew, James, and John were local fishermen. From what we can tell from history and the biblical account, they were most likely working small family-owned businesses. Peter and Andrew were brothers, as were James and John. Their counterparts today would be involved in the predominant local industry of your area. In my home state of Oklahoma, they might be ranchers. Their spread would be small, a family-owned enterprise in which sons follow Dad into a multi-generational trade.

* Matthew was a tax collector. His job was both financial and political, and he was among the most distrusted businessmen of his time. Perhaps in our society today, he might have been an IRS auditor or a politician.

* Simon was a political zealot. Do you have any of those in your church? I do. They are a peculiar bunch, cause-oriented, ready to suffer misunderstanding or worse for their beliefs. Although they can fly off the handle, they are great motivators and are valuable to your group.

* Judas Iscariot was the betrayer. It is hard to fathom how anyone could have spent three years with the Master and still betray Him. As amazing as it seems, we, too, will have those among us who look great, act like disciples, but have different motivations than we do and who will eventually turn away. Don't be discouraged. If Jesus had this situation to deal with, who are we to expect less?

* Thomas, who we like to call "Doubting Thomas," is one of my favorites. I do not believe that he was so much doubting as demanding: demanding proof when it was available. Thomas was

not there when Jesus first appeared to the disciples after His res-
urrection, and Thomas was not going to accept on hearsay that
such a thing happened. After all, if it were true, he would stake his
very life on it.

There was another group like Thomas in the Bible commended
for this very attitude. Paul called the Bereans "more noble" than the
Thessalonians because the Bereans "examined the Scriptures every
day to see if what Paul said was true" (Acts 17:11). What was actually
happening was this: When Paul preached to them, they listened
carefully and then went home and studied to verify the message
they had been taught. They refused to base their lives on beliefs that
were someone's opinions (even if that someone was Paul). People
like this keep everyone in the group true to the Word; they demand
it. Pray that you will have a Thomas in your group.

The other original Twelve are mysteries in many ways, and that
is how God wanted it, I'm sure. It is good that everything is not
obvious. We depend more on God that way, and the journey
becomes an adventure.

Paul, an apostle chosen after Christ's ascension, was a tent-
maker. He was originally born into prestige and position and was
filled with pride to match his innumerable talents. After his conver-
sion on the Damascus road, his transformed character became a
tremendous witness for Christ for many generations since. He took
up tent making, both to support his church-planting ministry and
to identify with the common people with whom he lived. His usual
plan was to move into an area and stay for a considerable length of

time — in some cases, years. By the time he departed, he left a self-sustaining church in his wake.

Paul is both a model and an example to us. His model is duplicated in our day by the many missionaries, church planters, and pastors who work both in full-time professional ministry and hold jobs in the marketplace, supporting themselves and their ministries.

His example shows us today how ministry in the marketplace is made more effective by the Christian's work ethic of excellence. Tent making was an important occupation in the first century, not only because the Bedouins were dependent on finely crafted tents but also because the local "stores" were actually tents set up along the road. If a basket weaver had a leaky tent, his entire livelihood was at stake. So a good tent maker was a sought-after businessman who could be a tremendous witness for God if he was excellent at his work. The same is true in the twenty-first century.

Each of the apostles were chosen, trained, and sent out as ambassadors for the gospel. And what did Jesus do about women who wished to be included? Even though it would have been inappropriate in His day for women to be included among the Twelve He kept with Him constantly, Jesus valued and chose women. We know from both biblical and historical accounts that many people, including women, followed Jesus almost everywhere He went, probably setting up camp and cooking as the nomadic group traveled around the country.

We are very familiar with the changed lives and loyalty of such women as Mary Magdalene, whom Jesus rescued out of prostitution and who stayed with Him to the very end. We are told in Matthew that she was present at the Crucifixion: "There were many women there, looking on from a distance, who had followed Jesus from Galilee and helped him" (Matthew 27:55, TEV). Mary Magdalene was present when Jesus' body was laid in the tomb (see Matthew 27:61), and she was blessed to be the first person to whom Jesus showed Himself in His resurrected body (see Mark 16:9).

THE INVITATION

With Jesus' precedent in mind, begin to call each leader. Invite these men and women to breakfast or lunch at restaurants near their workplaces. Try to meet with two or three at each meal. The commitment that you will ask for will not be small. Each leader should make a pledge to try the group for nine months. Incidentally, this should not be an official program of the church and therefore should not be announced publicly.

Share with them that God has spoken to you about helping them in their ministries with the people they work with every day. Tell them that you will personally help them and a small group of others to focus on their passion to know and love Christ and to identify their spiritual gifts and talents. With the group's interaction, you will enable them to identify opportunities on the job to observe the needs of coworkers, become sensitive to them, and learn to listen to their hearts. Let the leaders know that the group will work to discover ways that they can serve their superiors, their peers, their customers, their associates, and those who work for them. In this group, you plan to be only the facilitator and spiritual mentor, not the teacher. In fact, you are aware that if you do much more than ask leading questions, you could kill the creativity of it.

With this kind of introduction, these first get-togethers should go very well. You will be heartened that many of the leaders enthusiastically want to participate. They will particularly appreciate that the focus is on their places of service, not yours. They will be pleased that you are taking the time out of your busy schedule to meet with them.

Of the possible fifteen leaders on your list, you may have only gotten twelve to a breakfast or lunch. Even if two of them cannot make the time to participate for the next nine months and two others have conflicts, you could still have eight leaders agree to be in the group. These hypothetical numbers may be high; it is worth the effort, even if your group numbers two — you and one other.

YOUR FOCUS

In the last chapter, I talked about Jesus seeking out workplace leaders and starting to build relationships. As the Twelve spent time "with Jesus" they slowly began to understand and to build long-term relationships. The purpose of these relationships was not to be an end in itself but a platform from which the Twelve would be "sent out." The focus of your group of leaders is to be outward as well.

Let me share a story and a particular question that you could use as the focus of your small group. This question could dramatically shift the focus of your ministry.

One day a pastor drove in from another state to join me for lunch and some time together. As I listened to the discouraged pastor, I silently prayed, *Lord, please give me the words to help this man. I am just a businessman, and it is hard for me to comprehend all that he is facing.* My heart went out to him as he shared that both he and his people were overworked just keeping all the activities of the small church in place. I asked him to tell me about several of the key leaders in his church. He explained that one was an engineer at a large aircraft manufacturing plant and another was a CPA who had an accounting practice. God immediately gave me the question that has been the breakthrough to helping hundreds of pastors across the country.

I told this pastor that he needed to go to the engineer and ask him this question: "What can I do to help you have a ministry with the other engineers and coworkers at your plant?" I explained that the growth of the church would take care of itself if he first began to care for and equip his people. We began to visualize small groups of engineers meeting throughout the plant, studying the Bible, praying together, and sharing their lives with each other.

We then turned to the CPA. These accounting professionals may be the most overworked people during the months prior to the tax deadline. However, besides a pastor or a physician, the accountant is the one person that many people go to when they face the crises of life. I recommended that the pastor go to the CPA with the same question. We began to visualize the CPA sharing Christ with clients facing marital problems, financial difficulties, long-term illness, and even death.

A few months after this encounter, I was speaking at an evangelism and leadership seminary event sponsored by Leighton Ford. I was there to represent the workplace and give the participants an understanding of the marketplace leaders in their congregations. We wanted to help these pastors to better relate to their laity and become proficient at equipping them.

After sharing several of my own life experiences and some scriptural principles, I asked the class the same question that I had asked the struggling pastor:

"Have any of you ever asked the key leaders in your church how you could help them to have a ministry in the unique work situations in which God has sovereignly placed them?"

The silence was deafening. Then we began a lively and lengthy discussion on how each of us could return to our local churches or ministries and begin to ask that question. Since then, I have personally asked many pastors this question; I also have quizzed business leaders across our country about whether or not they had ever been asked a similar question. Over 95 percent of both groups normally respond in the negative. You can start to change all that.

As you begin to form your group, ask God how you could use this simple question to multiply the ministry of the Holy Spirit through those in your church. Remember, you are not recruiting this group of leaders to the church's activities or to your ministry, but you are asking them to allow you to help them be used by God where they are.

The following is a real-life example of how a friend of mine named John Crawford lives out the "How may I help you?" philosophy. Over eighty years old, John has been at discipling so long that he doesn't care to add people to a structure, a chart, or a report — he just wants to help them where they are.

Mike was a schoolteacher in a small town a couple of hours away from where John lived. In his earlier years, Mike had been active helping others spiritually, but with the pressure of work, raising a family, and caring for his parents, the ministry had lost focus. Though Mike was eager to drive to the city to see John, John insisted on driving out to see Mike. It made a huge impression on Mike that John wanted to "come to his turf" and help him, not recruit him to a ministry.

For several years John drove to Mike's town and spent time with him. Eventually, Mike began to help three men in his church in their walks with Christ. John often met with Mike and his disciples. Mike began to reproduce disciples and now has produced to the third and fourth generation.

Sometimes pastors think that they must do all or most of the work. Perhaps God wants you to pick up a few leaders along the way and give yourself away to their ministries. Every church has several eager "Mikes" waiting for someone to invest in them. They are looking for someone who sees them as valuable in the environment where God has placed them.

Be someone who will ask the question "How may I help you?" This question will give your group its focus.

THE GOALS OF THE GROUP

In Mark 3, we saw Jesus selecting the Twelve. (As we know, it took

Him three years to get them equipped to do the ministry on their own. Even then, they had to learn to depend fully on the Holy Spirit.) In Mark 4, Jesus wasted no time in challenging them to be reproducing ministers. They were to be like good soil that produces up to one hundredfold (see verse 8). The disciples were to be light-bearers (see verse 21) and, like a small mustard seed, would become large plants (see verse 32). Jesus was preparing the Twelve so that one day they would be ready to multiply His ministry around the world. Your objective for your group should be identical to that of Jesus.

Let me share possible goals that you might adopt:

First, that the leaders would focus more on their personal relationship with Christ throughout their day; second, that they would look at each contact in the workplace as a divine appointment to show God's love (not necessarily in a religious manner); and finally, that each leader would be sensitive to God's working in the lives of others and look for intentional and spontaneous opportunities to share Christ.

These, of course, are not the only goals that you might consider using. They are just starting points for your thinking. Tailor your group's goals to the vision God gives you.

THE FIRST SESSION

Your group's first meeting may be met with both apprehension and expectancy. Most of these leaders have never been in a group that focused not only on their spiritual growth but also on ministry in their sphere of influence. At the first session, discuss the format for future meetings. Consider a time of sharing and prayer, a time for studying a passage from God's Word specifically as it applies to the workplace leader's spiritual life or spiritual ministry, and a time for reporting progress and strategy on how each leader can positively impact coworkers. The group should jointly decide how much study should be required during the week. Again, structure it to meet your group's specific personality.

Here is a good exercise to end the first session that might help the group visualize its philosophy and purpose. Ask each leader to simply place his or her Bible in one hand and his or her weekly calendar in the other. Then have them ask God's Holy Spirit to give them wisdom as they try to integrate the two. Yes, God is working a new focus into their lives. It centers on Him, on people, and completely surrounds the marketplace of thirsting people who do not know that Jesus Christ is the only answer.

MEET REGULARLY

During the first few sessions you should purposely seek to be vulnerable. You may have never done this before. Yes, you have led many small groups, taught, and preached comfortably behind the pulpit. But this is different. You may not have the answers for each of their situations. The problems may not always be white or black. Many of these leaders deal with the gray every day. Being a disciple of Jesus in the workplace is not easily defined and the results are hard to measure. All you have is God's Word, His empowering Spirit, and each other.

As the group meets every week or every other week, challenge each member to be more caring, encouraging, and loving toward coworkers. As the leader, you will help them learn to do these things as a lifestyle. Model these attitudes and actions to the group by your own relationship with them. Teach them not to get discouraged when people do not respond or even notice the attention, time, and efforts being made. Encourage them to persist, be patient, and wait on the Holy Spirit to work in the lives of their coworkers.

The entire time this is going on, you will be building into this group of people. Many of them will, for the first time, be integrating their spiritual life and their work life. Sunday will finally become relevant to Tuesday afternoon. These meetings will not be a time of your preaching to them, but a time of sharing, asking questions, and praying. As God answers those prayers and works through those men and women, their faith will grow and their expectations will increase accordingly. It is amazing to see the power of God as He accomplishes His will.

HOW IT MIGHT LOOK

Let me give a hypothetical example of what a meeting might look like and how you might prepare for it. Let's theorize that you have a group of eight leaders — six men and two women — who have decided to meet weekly for breakfast and study at Mason's office. Mason will supply donuts and coffee, and they will spend one hour together.

In preparation, you open your Bible. John 15 is a chapter that is familiar; you have undoubtedly preached on it many times. It has great topics for business leaders, and you have picked verse 12 as a focal point for this week. Last week, during the first session, you asked all of them to read the whole chapter several times during the week, paying attention to verse 12 and asking themselves, *How do I love others in my workplace?*

The members arrive promptly at 6:30 A.M., looking sleepy but expectant. Your ground rules have been simple: Come when you are in town, be prepared and prompt, and keep confidences as a vow to God. This week, one member is out of town on business and another is not there, but six are accounted for. First, you ask Jennifer to lead in prayer. Then you may want to briefly ask each member how the week went and what issues he or she is facing. You could take some time now or at the end of the hour to get a prayer request from each member. I write them on 3 x 5 cards and take them home to remind me to pray. You may want to record them in a journal.

Next, you ask David to read John 15:9-15 aloud. You may want to read more of the passage, but I recommend that you keep it short. Have him reread verse 12. Then ask, "What does it mean to love people where we work? How do we do this?" Let the discussion begin, using leading questions as necessary to guide the discussion.

Andy may say that this is difficult for him. He works in a high-pressure medical environment, and there is not much love there. You ask the members to share ways that Andy can show Christ's love. Force them to be specific. If no one contributes, you may ask Andy directly, "Thinking about the people you will be with today, which people do you know have needs?" The others should soon join in. Jennifer responds that everyone has needs, so Andy's job is to identify the needs that he can help meet, with God's wisdom. Ryan suggests that such needs are likely to be fairly common to all: issues with health, children, parents, marriage, and finances. Andy remembers that there is a young nurse who lost her grandmother last week. He can minister to this grieving coworker by sending a card and offering to pray for her.

Next, you go to Glenda. She has a coworker who is always negative and complaining. The guy is certainly not lovable. You ask, "Does Jesus really expect us to *love* that kind of person?" The group begins to strategize about how Glenda can love the guy who only seems to want to make everyone around him miserable. This project will not be completed quickly.

Ryan shares about a supplier who is not doing a good job as a subcontractor. The group discusses how to confront the supplier in the right way, with Christ's love. Next, Mason declares that he has a customer who is not dealing with integrity. He is demanding that Mason's firm buy supplies from a specific supplier at excessive prices. Mason has learned that the firm is owned by the customer's wife. "How do you show love to a dishonest person?" The group decides to spend an entire week on this subject.

Finally, David is concerned about a former coworker who is out of work and really needs a job. David believes that the man is not a Christian, and he sees this as an opportunity to show Christ's love. He asks for suggestions from the group. In each case, you try to elicit input from as many members as possible.

Cut off the discussion at an hour so that you can end on time. One or two members decide to continue their discussion during lunch tomorrow or over breakfast later in the week. The assignment for next week comes again from John 15 — verses 4, 5, and 16. The questions to ponder are, "What does fruit look like in the context of your job? Is spiritual fruit visible?"

There are several other workplace topics in John 15. You might ask, "What does it look like to obey Christ's commands in the work-place?" or "Does Jesus really intend for us to experience joy in the daily workplace, even with an unreasonable employer?"

Remember:

* Lead and guide the discussion; do not teach.
* Get as many people as possible involved in the dialogue.
* Encourage vulnerability, and do not become critical of past deci-sions or judgmental as people bring up dilemmas.
* After a few weeks, rotate the leadership. You should still lead 50 percent of the time, but the others can learn to facilitate as you have done. That takes some time demand from you, although you are still there to mentor and spiritually guide.

FANNING THE FLAME

It will take six, twelve, or even eighteen months for the fire to start. When it does start, you will never be able to put it out. These lead-ers will finally understand how they are to relate to nonChristian coworkers. They will learn how to be sensitive, listen, and become available. They will learn to become servant leaders and caring encouragers. It will even help their marriages. They will learn how to share their faith when the Holy Spirit has prepared the way. They will understand that the secular becomes spiritual when done for the eternal. The leaders will get excited about what God is doing in their lives, within the group, within the church, and in the workplace. They will see God at work, even in the most improbable coworker. The long-term results are limited only by the imagination of the Holy Spirit.

This ministry can more than double the scope and outreach of your church. The new Christians from the workplace may join a church across town or in another city. They could join yours. This simple process will form valuable relationships, break down barriers between the clergy and laity, build leaders, create opportunities for evangelism, and make people sensitive to God's Spirit at work in those around them.

Just as Jesus did with His disciples, you will have to explain various principles to your leaders each week. You will likely want to assign a passage or a topic ahead of time. At times, you may choose to use a book or other printed materials. The more you can get the leaders to discover for themselves, the more beneficial it will be. At the back of this book, Appendix 1 consists of issues that typically arise in the workplace, which you can use to plan your sessions. Appendix 2 lists sources of materials and other resources.

ACTION STEPS

1. Finalize your list of potential group members.

2. Spend plenty of time praying for these people.

3. Personally enlist the members.

4. Set a starting date, day, time, and place for the first meeting.

5. Determine the goals of the group.

IT WAS HE WHO GAVE
SOME TO BE APOSTLES,

SOME TO BE
PROPHETS,
SOME TO BE EVANGELISTS,

AND SOME TO BE

PASTORS
AND TEACHERS,
TO PREPARE GOD'S
PEOPLE FOR WORKS OF

SERVICE.

—EPHESIANS 4:11-12

CHAPTER III

THE PASTOR AS EQUIPPER

AS MENTIONED IN the last chapter, soon after Jesus called the Twelve, He began to explain to them that they were to be ministers who reproduced dramatically. What is the ministry that God has called all of us as believers to do? What does it mean to be a minister in the workplace? *Ministry* is a broad term and is often misunderstood. I would define it as "participation in the work of God with an eternal motivation." It is not a question of the activity or vocation, but of the *focus*. If we have an eternal focus, then we can participate with Jesus Christ in the work of reconciliation in a person's life or in the work of sanctification and maturity in the life of a fellow believer.

EQUIPPING FOR THE MINISTRY

Ministry must have as its long-term eternal focus either evangelism or discipleship as defined by Jesus in the Great Commission (see Matthew 28:19-20). Ministry has as its goal to enlarge and mature the body of Christ. Is feeding the hungry a ministry? Yes, if its focus is eternal. But if it is only to fill empty stomachs, then it is just a good deed. So, ministry is determined not just by *what* we do but *why* we do it. This has caused huge confusion in our churches. Some ministries start out with an eternal focus, but lose their vitality when they become just other activities of doing good works.

The "religious" works that I do, if done for temporal reward or glory, are not ministry. Conversely, the secular job that I perform, if done with an eternal focus, can actually involve ministry to members of Christ's body as well as unbelievers. As a good friend of mine, Walter Henrichsen, has often said, "The secular becomes spiritual if done for the eternal, and the spiritual or religious becomes secular if done for the temporal." The work of God cannot be created, measured, or controlled. We choose to join God in His work in those around us. He allows us to join Him and to minister to or serve others.

The term *ministry* is used more than thirty times in the New Testament. The apostles ministered the Word (see Acts 6:4). We, as ambassadors for Christ, are involved in the ministry of reconciliation (see 2 Corinthians 5:18). Paul challenged Timothy to discharge the duties of his ministry (see 2 Timothy 4:5). Ministry is the calling, the privilege, and the responsibility of *every* member of the body of Christ. Sadly, many church members today don't fully understand this truth. Do your people understand that they are full-time ministers of Jesus Christ?

We must redistribute the ministry load from our overburdened clergy to the laity. But, in the transition, much of the eternally useless activities need to be eliminated. For instance, examine church committees. Is each one still a ministry, or has it lost its focus over time? Could many of them be eliminated or reduced in size in order to free up more frontline troops? We seem to be an army with 90 percent of our soldiers behind the line.

Notice again that this ministry is every Christian's, not just yours. This may be a shock, but God never intended for you, as a pastor, to do this ministry alone. You are to assist the saints in the ministry that God has called them to, wherever they are. That is a huge paradigm shift in thinking. The ministry is God's; we are to work together with Him (see 2 Corinthians 6:1; 1 Corinthians 3:9).

As you equip your people to become ministers, help them to become sensitive to the lost, to learn to listen to them, and to boldly share the good news with them. Teach your people to serve, not to be served. Equip them for battle and do not baby them; you are preparing these saints for spiritual warfare (see Ephesians 6). Do not cater to those who are rich or powerful or who are in positions of authority. Tell them the truth about sin, discipleship, and maturity.

Until the mature saint lives out the gospel in his family, work-place, and neighborhood, he has not been adequately equipped. If we ran a college only teaching the students to become teachers at the college without sending them off-campus to compete in life, our college would be a failure. Ministry is not so much attending a church activity as it is training one's children, serving one's neighbor, listening to an unbelieving coworker's questions on real-life issues, or leading other businesspeople in a Bible study.

Are we pulling our people out of the world, or are we renewing their minds and sending them back into their world (see John 17:18)? While you are sending them out, why don't you join them?

Visit them in their Jerusalem and in their Judea. Visit their offices, schools, and factories.

I sometimes think that our churches are like basic training centers that never graduate a class. In fact, some of them have confused the training arena with the battlefield. What percentage of your church's ministry takes place outside its walls? If you are honest, the answer might surprise you.

You, as a pastor, are equipping your people to minister for Jesus Christ in the marketplace, medical complexes, high-tech centers, educational systems, halls of government, financial markets, and every walk of life. You are equipping them to be ministers of the kingdom (see Mark 4:11). God's kingdom is not limited by the boundaries of race, class, age, sex, or denomination. God is into reproduction and He has chosen to do that through people.

A Leadership Network forum on the twenty-first century was summarized by the Net Fax, which addressed this subject:

> Equipping and deploying people for service and ministry is a significant movement of God and part of a larger shift in the role of the church leadership from doing to equipping. It is not a program, nor is it "church work." It is not about "filling slots" or assessing tools. It is about people. It is about discovering . . . their gifts, talents, passions, stories, and needs and then equipping them and releasing them to be the body of Christ in their communities and the world.

The forum addressed several critical elements to lay mobilization, including "a buy-in to equipping people for ministry on the part of the senior pastor," who also has to "cast the vision for equipping" and "model it in his own ministry." One leader at the forum observed that, "This is not a 'quick fix' or a 'program,' but a foundation and value that undergirds every ministry in the life of our church, and it just takes time."[1]

Wayne Cordeiro, author of *Doing Church As a Team*, challenges us to view Ephesians 4 not just as a suggestion for an equipping church but also as a mandate from God.

> Pastors have a responsibility to equip the people for ministry rather than do the ministry. After leaders are identified, they must be "involved" and "have an opportunity" to be released in ministry. I wonder why we got into our current mess — because the laity wanted the paid professionals to do the work, or because the clergy were reluctant to let us (the laity) do it? Regardless of the cause, we must change our thinking and take equipping seriously.[2]

In our surveys of the laity over the years, we have received some frank answers.

In one questionnaire we asked them, "What specific things could a church staff member do to help you make your personal ministry more effective?"

Lance, who was at that time a businessman but is now a pastor, said, "Teach spiritual gifts and their practical application. Encourage ministry development, even if it is 'outside' the church umbrella. Train in marketplace ministry."

Warren said, "Develop a plan and practice of helping church leaders to become effective Christians in the context of their daily sphere of activities. View the local church as a facilitator of the ministries of the individual members of the body rather than as an end in itself."

Although these quotes are just a sampling of many, it is obvious that business leaders who want to witness for God realize that their primary spheres of influence are outside of the church walls and that they need pastoral help to be effective there.

My experience with God-fearing businesspeople is that they want to partner with their pastors and would greatly value their help.

THE PASTOR/EQUIPPER AS A SHEPHERD

After leaving seminary, some graduates will have apostolic ministries. They will plant churches and start other ministries in new places. Others will go out and have prophetic ministries. They will proclaim the light of God's truth in a darkened world. Still others will be evangelists like Phillip (see Acts 21:8). But the majority of seminary graduates have been called by God to be pastors/teachers, or the term used most often in Scripture, *shepherds*. God promises, "Then I will give you shepherds after my own heart, who will lead you" (Jeremiah 3:15). Luke writes, "The Holy Spirit has made you overseers. Be shepherds of the church of God, which he bought with his own blood" (Acts 20:28). Peter reminds us to "be shepherds of God's flock that is under your care . . . eager to serve" (1 Peter 5:2).

God has called every pastor to be a shepherd of God's flock — to protect, to lead, to care for. Pastors are to be servants of Christ's body and teachers of the saints. Most pastors have a sincere heart for God and want desperately to *teach* God's Word. But unless you first become a shepherd, you cannot be an effective teacher.

Shepherds are patient, aggressively protective, and constantly on the alert for dangers to the sheep and to themselves. Although sheep are extremely loyal, they are also timid and helpless; therefore, the shepherd must first earn their trust by his actions.

Pastors, like shepherds, must learn to understand the laity's needs, become sensitive and available to them, actively listen to them, encourage them, and communicate effectively with them. Your servant heart, your brokenness, and your prayer life will be more important than your preaching.

Glenn Wagner's comments, which I've adapted here, are insightful:

> Shepherding is primarily relational. This is the difference between the pastor as merely a leader, and a shepherd. One cannot be a shepherd without being in relationship to the sheep. Leaders have no such mandate. Secular models of leadership, if adopted by the pastor, see people as a *product*, not as a *priority*. Such leaders are engineers, not encouragers; manag-

ers, not ministers.

Shepherding encompasses leadership, including all the variations thereof. In the postmodern era, the shepherd model is less a strategic ploy as it is a poetic response to the searching of an aimless, straying culture. Postmodern people have technology; they don't need another CEO or more gee-whiz gadgetry. They need shepherds who will provide care, concern, courage, and commitment to the flock.

If you're feeling the stress of ministry, perhaps it's time to look again at the shepherd model. You don't hear of too many shepherds stressing out; they know that all they have to do is take care of the sheep.[3]

UNDERSTANDING THE MARKETPLACE LEADERS AMONG US

Before you get the idea that shepherding is a quiet activity among gentle and obedient sheep, let's be realistic. Having workplace leaders in your congregation feels like someone let a bunch of horses into the fold. They don't act the same as sheep, and sometimes they ignore the usual boundaries and ways of doing things. They even sleep standing up! There are stallions and mares of all ages, colors, and sizes. Examining this species we find there are leaders, executives, and entrepreneurs.

Leaders of all types have certain things in common. People follow them. They like having control. They can be of any personality type, but are usually a commanding presence whose opinion is always considered by the group. They may make others feel nervous or intimidated, especially those whose opinions differ. On the flip side, they are consistent finishers and dependable decision makers.

Entrepreneurs are a unique bunch; they are the wildest of the horses. Though leadership can be learned, entrepreneurs are born and exhibit from an early age the traits that make them distinctive. Foremost among these is the vision to do what hasn't been done before. For example, my dad, Jack, a classic entrepreneur, took eggs on the bus with him when he traveled to school from his small rural town to another small rural town. Why? Because eggs were more expensive in the second town, and he found that he could sell eggs there and make a profit.

By age fourteen, Jack had left home and was on his own in the world. He coped without fear because entrepreneurs are basically fearless. Visionaries who actually accomplish their visions, they think they can figure their way out of anything (or into anything), and they usually do it. They are extremely self-reliant and opinionated and want to be in control. They see the big picture and make good delegators (because they do not want to be burdened with the details). By the time he was twenty, Jack had graduated from college, had a commission from the Army, and had been married for two years.

All three of Jack's sons are leaders, but not all of them are entrepreneurs. I, however, am one. I used to buy five-cent candy and sell it for ten cents at my brothers' peewee baseball games. I never could figure out why they didn't catch on and bring their own candy, but they didn't, so I kept selling it. Entrepreneurs will try anything.

They figure that if 50 percent of their ideas work, they are way ahead. I paid for the gas and repairs for my first car by taking my high school friends to school in any weather — I charged their parents the same amount they would pay for bus service. Most entrepreneurs know that to succeed, a deal must be win/win.

Entrepreneurs tend to never retire. They may sell their company, but new ideas are always luring them into a new field. They will usually start a new company after "retirement." This means that as older men and women, they are still active (mentally and physically) and available to you as the pastor. When examining the spiritual gifting of an entrepreneur, he or she will look immediately like an administrator or leader but may actually be an exhorter or prophet. Be careful when helping these members find their gifting; their strong personalities and activities can mask their underlying God-given strengths.

Business owners are another type of horse. True entrepreneurs usually own their own business, will eventually, or have in the past. But one can be a business owner and not be an entrepreneur. This person may have inherited the business or bought an existing one. The business owner still has distinct traits. He or she has a strong, driven personality and can be an intimidating presence in a group. He or she tends to be organized and thrives on getting the details right. He or she can be a micromanager, a tendency that can drive you crazy at times.

All of these leaders flourish when they are in charge. Although they sound pretty powerful, and they can be, they also have their own insecurities. They may feel intimidated by their pastor or by other leaders. Unless the Holy Spirit has tempered them, they may try to bluff their way through circumstances in which they feel insecure by either acting confident when they aren't or being bossy. They hate to admit they don't have answers or that they don't know what to do. They are normal people with strengths and weaknesses, just like everyone else, but their strengths and weaknesses happen to be more obvious. Understanding them changes your expectations as a pastor, which leads to less confusion and frustration with them.

Church members may ask you to do many things: create programs, enlarge facilities, increase attendance, and come to the hospital, graveside, or wedding altar. They want you to preach powerfully, make them feel comfortable, be available at all times, keep the church machinery running, make them feel good, and even win souls. But God has not asked you to major on these things — He has asked you to equip the body of believers. You are to develop mature saints out of timid sheep. That sounds like Mission Impossible to me, but we know that through Christ all things are possible (see Philippians 4:13).

Many pastors are tired from doing all of the aforementioned tasks, but the exhaustion doesn't come from equipping. Equipping is hard work and demands a lot of energy, but it is energizing, rewarding, and satisfying. Note that God picks out your flock and has given you the responsibility of shepherding it. You are not to build a church institution but an army of finely trained soldiers. You are not to grow an organization but a living, breathing organism — the body of Christ. You are not just to encourage the saints but have been asked by God to equip them. You are not just to inspire them but also to prepare them for battle. You, as a pastor, have not been called by God to establish larger budgets or better facilities but to build stronger saints. I am not saying that a big, organized, well-budgeted church is not valuable or important. Nor am I underestimating the time demanded of you to "run" it. I am talking about motives and priorities. I am saying that heading a church organization is not the goal; it is not the reason God called you to pastor.

Remember, this work of equipping the saints is God's work. He is the good Shepherd (see John 10), the Chief Shepherd (see 1 Peter 5), and the great Shepherd (see Hebrews 13). He is the Shepherd of our soul (see 1 Peter 2). He began the work and He will finish it. The pastor is His undershepherd, His assistant. Scripture says, "He who began a good work in you will carry it on to completion" (Philippians 1:6) and explains, "May... our Lord Jesus, that great Shepherd of the sheep, equip you with everything good for doing his will" (Hebrews 13:20-21). Yes, Jesus Christ is the Master Equipper.

THE QUALITIES OF THE EQUIPPER

The root of the word *equip* is translated this way only once in the New Testament. (The *New International Version,* the *New American Standard Bible,* and *The New Testament in Modern English* use the word *equip*; *The Amplified Bible* adds *strengthen*; and the *King James Version* uses *perfect*.) However, the root word is used fifteen times in the New

Testament with the idea of "to make fit" or "to prepare fully." First Corinthians 1:10 and 2 Corinthians 13:9 (NASB) use the phrase "be made complete," implying a process leading to consummation. First Peter 5:10 promises us that God "will Himself perfect...you" (NASB). As a pastor, you must prepare the ministers (the saints) to do their work, teach them the truth of God's Word, help them to overcome their problems, allow them to develop their skills, and give them a vision for reaching out to others. It is a process.

MODEL-ORIENTED

The key to equipping is modeling. Most of what we learn is observed — "caught" not "taught." Jesus said, "A disciple is not above his teacher, but when he is fully trained he will be like his teacher" (Luke 6:40, PH). Paul wrote, "Whatever you have learned or received or heard from me, or seen in me — put it into practice" (Philippians 4:9). The key to being an effective model is having your own deep, personal relationship with God. People will notice what you do publicly, but the success of a spiritual ministry lies in what you do privately.

PRIORITY-MOTIVATED

If you want to invest in workplace leaders whose ministry will withstand the test of time, you need to impress upon them the importance of keeping first things first — and, of course, you must do the same. They must get alone with God daily. They must plan times of personal refreshment. As a routine matter, they must schedule time daily, weekly, monthly, and annually with their spouse and children.

There may be a few exceptions, but normally, leaders who walk with God start their day with Him. Jesus constantly modeled this to His disciples. In Mark 1, we see Jesus ministering late into the evening. The whole city had gathered at the door (see verse 33). Do you, as a pastor, sometimes feel that way? Yet, according to verse 35, Jesus got up before dawn the next morning, went to a quiet place, and prayed. He often went to the mountains to pray (see Mark 6:46; Luke 6:12); He regularly prayed with or near His disciples (see Luke 9:18; 22:41). If Jesus, being fully God and fully man, needed this time with His Father, how much more do we need it today?

The most important thing you can do for your workplace leaders is to encourage them to set the alarm a few minutes early, spend personal time with God, and establish the habit of a solid devotional life. So many leaders have difficulty establishing this habit, and then they struggle throughout the day and wonder why. Workplace leaders often have so much talent and energy that they seek to "do life" in their own strength, demanding too much of themselves and others. Recommend that your leaders get a devotional book such as *My Utmost for His Highest*, by Oswald Chambers, and a modern paraphrase of Scripture such as *The New Living Translation* or *The Message*. Have them get a one-year Bible that provides an Old Testament and New Testament reading each day. These times in the Scriptures, prayer, and meditation will change their lives.

To gain strength and perspective, they also must schedule time for quietness and rest. Have them consider exercising and praying concurrently. I have made this a consistent habit in my life for more than twenty years. Prayer walks are good for the soul as well as the body.

A few days away from time to time will lead to weeks of clearer thinking. Spiritual recuperation, physical exercise, rest, and emotional and mental relaxation will pay great dividends to the leader.

Equip these men and women to face life's daily battles with the sword of the Spirit, God's Word. Equip them to not be satisfied with the pleasures of this world, but to have a passion for the lost. Equip them to know how to use their possessions as tools for the gospel, not as idols. Equip them to be stewards of God's resources and to avoid the bondage of debt. (Just because they are successful businesspeople does not mean that they know how to handle personal finances.) Equip them to bear much fruit, not just to come to the vineyard and eat, as they allow the Holy Spirit to work in and through them (see John 15).

ACTIVE LISTENER

Being a good listener is an active and learned skill. While doing it, we must rely on the Holy Spirit to enable us to hear not only people's words but their hearts as well. We must develop the skill of discerning the meaning behind words and in body movements. As you know, we can easily misunderstand each other. In order to be successful, communication involves thinking as we hear, then formulating thoughts, and finally sharing those thoughts. We tend to rush the process in our everyday lives. The following are suggestions for improving the skill of listening:

• Do not interrupt. Interrupting translates into, "What I want to say is more important than what you are saying."

* Interpret both words and emotions. Body language gives important clues. Clenched fists mean anger; crossed arms indicate defensiveness; eyes downcast can mean depression, guilt, or shame; and fidgeting reveals nervousness.
* Resist filtering; remain open-minded. Avoid judging or jumping to conclusions due to your own values.
* Summarize what you heard back to the speaker: "I think I heard you say . . ."
* Take your time wording your reply. Silence is not fatal.

TEACHER/FACILITATOR

You will be both teacher and facilitator during the equipping process. You must balance the times that you are teaching principles from God's Word with those times that you are letting others do most of the talking and brainstorming. At those times, you are the facilitator.

Let me close this chapter with some questions to ponder. If you preach and teach the Word of God in your church but the people do not get into the Word for themselves, have they been truly equipped (see Acts 17:11)? If we take our people on short-term mission trips across the world but they still see missions only as an activity rather than as a lifestyle, will they ever reach their "Jerusalem"? If we have evangelistic training and outreaches but our people do not naturally share their faith in their spheres of influence, have they really been equipped (see Philemon 1:6)? We must change our focus. Teaching can occur from the pulpit, but training occurs only in the trenches.

Are you ready to get involved in equipping leaders for their ministries?

When you leave your church — which one day you will — whether after three years or thirty, the only thing that will matter will be the lives of the men, women, and children you have impacted for eternity. The same is true for any business owner, CEO, or leader in the workplace.

ACTION STEPS

1. Take some time with your leaders and discuss the spiritual gifts, personality styles, and passions of each one. Discuss as a group how leaders can lead with different styles.

2. Brainstorm ways in which they could each serve their employees, leadership team, boss, customers, suppliers, and even competitors.

3. Ask each group member for one thing you could do to equip him or her to represent Christ and serve others in the workplace.

4. Give them an opportunity to strategize with each other on how they could impact their firms, their neighborhoods, their circles of influence, and even their entire workplace industries for Christ.

SO THE PHARISEES AND
TEACHERS OF THE LAW ASKED
JESUS, "WHY
DON'T YOUR DISCIPLES
LIVE ACCORDING TO THE TRADITION
OF THE ELDERS
INSTEAD OF EATING
THEIR FOOD WITH

'UNCLEAN' HANDS?"
AND HE SAID TO THEM:
"YOU HAVE A FINE WAY OF
SETTING ASIDE THE
COMMANDS OF GOD
IN ORDER TO OBSERVE YOUR
OWN TRADITIONS!"

—MARK 7:5,9

CHAPTER IV

OVERCOMING OBSTACLES TO WORKPLACE MINISTRY

～～ 〇

IF YOU HAVE been in the pastorate very long you must enjoy Mark 7, which records Jesus' big-time battle with the religious leaders concerning tradition. Whether a church is large or small, urban or rural, new or old, conservative or more moderate, it has its own set of traditions. The word *tradition* as defined by *Webster's Seventh New Collegiate Dictionary* is "the handing down of information, beliefs, and customs by word of mouth or by example from one generation to another."[1] Tradition is a marker to help identify families, groups, and cultures. It reinforces belief systems and values.

Jesus visited the temple and did not forsake most parts of Jewish tradition, but it definitely bothered the Pharisees that He did not keep all of their traditions. Jesus valued tradition when it accented doctrine, and, indeed, He instituted the tradition of Communion. When tradition, however, needed to be changed or was no longer necessary, He acted accordingly. Thus He picked corn ("worked") on the Sabbath when He and the disciples needed something to eat. It drove the Pharisees crazy.

Similarly, we have many good traditions in our churches and

families today. Some of these are valuable and need to be passed on to the next generation. However, we are easily caught up in traditional religious patterns that are neither scriptural nor meaningful, and there will always be Pharisees among us who want to defend them. When we cling to these, they create belief confusion and become obstacles. You, as pastor, must strip away the erroneous traditions that your workplace leaders rely on, so that they can deal with the heart issues before God. And if you personally struggle with any of these obstacles, then perhaps within this confidential small-group community, you can tackle them together.

There are at least four ways that you can deal with traditional religious beliefs: (1) continue to observe them, (2) ignore them, (3) change them, or (4) start something new. Jesus did not choose to observe many of the religious traditions; He knew that the end result would be lack of spiritual vibrancy and perhaps worse. He also did not choose to ignore them. We know that because if the Pharisees did not bring them into the conversation, Jesus would. Jesus could have been a crusader and tried to change them, but He chose not to change the system that was in place. Instead, Jesus started something new — investing in twelve disciples and emphasizing the principles of the kingdom.

Many workplace leaders are confused about their role in evangelizing the world. They often feel that their small part is insignificant compared to the contributions of the "professionals." They have resigned themselves to a "support" position in helping those professionals who have been trained, equipped, and gifted to be on the front lines. This is why many have lost a passion for the vision.

Let's look at a dozen obstacles, or traditional beliefs, that we have in our churches that keep workplace leaders from visualizing their mission as ambassadors for Jesus Christ.

1. We have confused a person's position with his spirituality.

Which is more spiritual: driving a church bus or a truck? Being a church administrator or vice president of a large firm? Being a minister of music or a school teacher? Being a missionary or working in a factory? Being a pastor or a salesperson?

Of course the answer is neither! Being spiritual is being in the will of God. When I was a teenager, I viewed spirituality as positions on a ladder. On the top rung was a missionary, next was a pastor, next was a Christian worker, and somewhere near the bottom was a businessman. I was wrong, but I nearly went into the pastoral ministry (when that was not where God wanted me) because I wanted my life to count for Christ. I had confused my "position" with my spirituality. Make sure that your leaders know that God calls them to full-time ministry in the workplace.

2. We have confused platform with ministry.

The average person has been led to believe that the most important ministry happens on the platform (teaching, preaching, making music, and other visible ministries). Richard Halverson, the late Presbyterian pastor and greatly respected chaplain of the United States Senate, maintains that the church's greatest impact is between Sundays:

It is assumed in our culture that the Church impacts society *primarily as an institution*, or a bureaucracy. As a matter of fact — and New Testament teaching, especially — the *institutional impact of the Church in the world is minimal. Where is the Church between Sundays* when the buildings are empty except for pastor and staff?

The Church is everywhere! Scattered, like seed and salt . . . penetrating all the neighborhoods, organizations, private clubs, etc. The impact of the institutional church on the culture is like dropping a saltshaker on food. In order to do its work, salt must be shaken from its container to make contact with the food . . . *disappearing as it penetrates.* When salt is doing its work, *it is invisible . . .* and the only way to measure its impact is by taste.

When Jesus told the parable of the wheat and tares, in explaining it He said, "The Son of Man is the sower, the field is the world, the good seed are the children of the Kingdom." In fact, in a series of parables concerning the Kingdom, Jesus insisted that the *Kingdom is invisible in the world* — like "treasure hidden in a field."

The real work of the Church takes place between Sundays — *when the Church is dispersed* — disappearing into the soil of the world around it. The impact of church institutions in the world is marginal. The *maximum impact* of the Church is when it is scattered — and invisible. And, incidentally, there is no way to measure this influence — no criteria. Jesus said that the wheat

and the weeds were not to be separated until the harvest.... And He said, "The harvest is the end of the age,
and the reapers are the angels" (Matthew 13:37-39).[2]

Let your leaders know that their platform in the workplace may be
more influential to a lost world than yours is.

3. We have confused the amount of time we spend with our level of commitment.

When new Christians become involved in more and more good
religious activities, they have less contact with the secular world,
except at their jobs. They may even spend less time with their
spouses and families. This time involvement normally increases
over a period of three to ten years, after which they may reach a time
of burnout and scale back. The church then loses some of these
young believers back to the secular world and some to casual Sunday
mediocrity. This is particularly true with leaders who must have a
passion and are prone to burnout.

The problem is not in the amount of time spent but in balancing
the time and opportunities that God has given us. Make sure that
your leaders understand that they are being ministers of God all day,
every day. Their performance on the job is just as important to God
as a religious activity.

4. We have confused teaching with training.

My good friend Charlie Riggs says, "Telling is not teaching, listening
is not learning; we learn to do by doing." *Telling* is simply giving a

command, such as, "John, I'd like for you to give your testimony at the meeting next Thursday." *Teaching* goes a step further by explaining how to do the job. "John, you can prepare your testimony by writing it out first. Then practice it to keep it no longer than five minutes. Include 'before,' 'during,' and 'after' parts in your salvation story." *Training* is interactive. "John, let's get together and talk about this. I'll show you how to write it out and practice with you."

Many workplace leaders are tired of eating overprocessed spiritual food, served by spoon-feeding. They want to learn how to feed themselves. They want to experience new situations and mine the treasures of God's Word for themselves. Our institutions have glamorized the communication process. Sophisticated videos, books, magazines, and performances have glorified the platform mentality. Our workplace leaders need more hands-on training, not just teaching. This takes time! Train your leaders, beginning with how to study the Bible on their own with just a Bible, paper, and a pen. Training involves them actually doing Bible study, doing evangelism, and discipling and serving others. Create this desire within them if it doesn't already exist.

5. We have confused size with significance.

Many of today's workplace leaders are not impressed by the size of our church budgets or facilities because they may deal in the corporate world with much larger budgets or facilities. They also are not impressed with our numbers, the geography we cover across the nation or across the world, or our political power struggles. But they do long to be involved in something significant because secular success in education, science, business, entertainment, politics, or any such endeavor is fleeting, and they know it.

People, leaders especially, want their lives to count for something, to leave a legacy. And they want to personally be in on the action, not just to "support" the efforts of the professionals. As my son, Lance, pastor of a Generation X church, explains, "Today's young leaders want to give themselves to a real spiritual vision that is bigger than they are. This causes them to rely on God!"

Do your leaders have the vision of God changing their workplace, their industry, their town or city?

6. We have expected them to come to us instead of us going to them.

When Jesus wanted to talk to the religious leaders, He went to the temple. But when He wanted to touch the lives of people who were hurting, He went to where they were (for example, He ministered to the Samaritan woman at the well where she drew water). And normally, when Jesus touched lives, He left them where He found them, so that they could impact others for Him. Rarely did He move them out of their circles of influence.

Have you ever noticed the people God called to be involved in something significant?

- When God wanted to reach out to Pharaoh, He chose Moses from a royal family.
- When God wanted to reach governors and kings, He chose the educated and religious Saul (later Paul).
- When He wanted to touch the lives of the common people, He

chose Peter, James, and John (fishermen).

* When He wanted to affect the leading politicians and tax collectors, He chose Matthew and Zaccheus.
* When looking for a way to reach the business community, He chose Barnabus and Lydia.

We must let our leaders understand that ministry can take place out in their marketplaces every day. You must be like Jesus and start something new. You must invest in each of the workplace leaders that God has given to you and help them to focus on the harvest field where God has placed them — the workplace.

Real workplace ministry is not taking religion, but rather the fragrance of Christ, to the office. It is not about activities but availability. Your leaders do not necessarily need to preach or pray on the job site but simply be salt and light. As they let Jesus live naturally through them, He will work though them to produce fruit in lives around them (see John 15:5). As they are unified and partner together, the world will see Jesus in them and finally understand God's love (see John 17:23).

In a recent article in "Modern Reformation," Marva Dawn presents the challenge:

> What would happen if everyone in our pews for worship on Sunday morning departed afterwards with a deep understanding of all that Jesus meant in John 15:16, "You did not choose me but I chose you. And I appointed you to go and bear fruit, fruit that

will last. . . ."? For that to happen, our worship would have to be remarkably filled with the sense that we did not choose to come, but that God is the Subject who has invited us here. Immersed in the wonder that God has chosen us for his purposes, appointed us specifically for our various ministries in the work, and equipped us to bear lasting fruit, we would depart with a vision for "being Church" the rest of the week. My greatest disagreement with those who advocate turning worship into the congregation's evangelistic tool is that this notion removes the responsibility of all the members for reaching out to their neighbors by being Church, by bearing the fruit of disciple-ship.[3]

Take a week on the fruit of the Spirit (see Galatians 5:22-23) and ask your group how they are exhibiting these characteristics.

7. We have confused our spiritual walk with Sunday church activities.

Your leaders must realize that Tuesday afternoon on the job is just as important to God as Sunday morning in corporate worship. When they focus wrongly, when they think that they can go and give on Sunday and then choose to do what they like the other six days of the week, they have bought into a lie.

Peter Senge, one of the revolutionary thinkers of our day, says, "I would argue that the mainstream of Christianity throughout the last 1,500 years, and particularly evident in the past 200 years, has been for the majority of practitioners, not a practice-oriented religion, but a Sunday religion, a religion of 'do what you want as long as you subscribe to the right things and you show up on Sunday to keep the institution going.'"4

One exercise you might consider is pairing up your leaders and having them call each other on Tuesday at 2 P.M. or Thursday at 10 A.M. to remind their partner that they are ministering at that very moment — for good or not.

Those workplace leaders must not segment their life into the sacred and the secular but realize that every activity is part of one's walk with God. Jim Craddock, founder of Scope Ministries, explained this concept well:

> As Christians we inhabit two worlds, the spiritual and the natural. One has to do with the things of God, the other with the things of man. I think this is the reason why Christians have polarized the sacred and the secular in their thinking.
>
> Unfortunately, the polarization of the sacred and the secular has caused a great deal of confusion among Christians. We view our church activity, our devotional time, our Bible study as sacred, and the rest of our activities as secular. One is viewed as a blessing, the other as a duty. This is most unfortunate for it causes problems in our Christian walk that ought not to be there. It is easy to let God be God in the sacred,

but because we have separated the two, our tendency is not to let God be God in the secular. We allow God to rule the sacred while we rule the secular.

What must be done is to view all that we do as sacred. We must come to the realization that our jobs, our relationships, and our activities are just as much an act of worship as our prayers and praise. Think upon this for a moment. The implications are enormous. I no longer need to be ashamed of who I am or what I do. My life, all of it, becomes a sacrament, an outward expression of an inward work of grace.[5]

Every work duty is sacred if done with a Christlike attitude. Every phone call, visit, and project is an invitation to join Him to touch another life.

Pastors must equip leaders to seize opportunities to share Christ with hurting people. It is not as much a question of "boldness" to proclaim as it is "willingness" to listen to the wounded. Jesus tells us that the harvest is plentiful, but the workers are few (see Matthew 9:36-38). Perhaps we have overemphasized the value of materials and programs and underemphasized the value of an individual sold out for Christ. Please do not misunderstand what I am saying here: There is importance and a place for materials and programs. I have used tracts, booklets, and other materials successfully in the workplace, but coworkers basically respond to caring, sensitive people.

8. We have focused on the institution instead of the individual.
As I noted at the beginning of this chapter, the Pharisees and religious leaders had this same problem in Jesus' day. Jesus warned them, "You have let go of the commands of God and are holding on to the traditions of men" (Mark 7:8). In his book *Leadership That Works*, Leith Anderson makes distinctions between yesterday's and today's priorities. He explains the shift from institutional to individual, from church to family, from duty to opportunity, from showing up to significance, and from faithfulness to effectiveness.[6] The leaders in your church, as individuals, want to have opportunities in which they can use their gifts and be effective and significant. They want to be able to participate in these while not neglecting their family. Have you adjusted to this shift?

9. We have confused reputation with servanthood.
If our leaders ever gain a platform to minister in the workplace, it will be because of their service to others, not their reputation. Len Sweet calls this "authenticity by participation, not professional credentials." Sweet goes on to say, "It is the anointing of the Spirit."[7] Leroy Armstrong, speaking to church leaders said, "The church has an unemployment problem. Too many saints are not being employed and deployed in ministry."[8] He is exactly right, as the age of representation has given birth to the age of participation.

As Margaret Wheatley said,

> The key trait of leadership today is having more confidence in other people than you have in yourself.

Shine the light on others. Ask them to participate. The ultimate in leadership today is not asking, "What kind of a world are our leaders creating?" but "How are our leaders helping us create the world we want to live in?" This issue of leadership today is not "What kind of story are our leaders writing for us?" but "How are our leaders helping me to write my own story?" Not "What are our leaders doing for me?" but "How are our leaders helping me to lead?" Preaching is not "How do I craft a better sermon?" but "How do I build a better congregation of participants?"9

Are you, as a pastor, continuing to polish your professionalism, or are you becoming a servant of participants (see Luke 20:46; Matthew 19:30)? Ask your leaders to do an act of service each day for a week at the office or at home without saying a word. Ask them to report on the results the following week.

10. We have focused on escaping the secular culture instead of invading it.

Ministry today is less about "segregation" and more about "penetration." Len Sweet addresses this problem: "Dealing with this new world and the church's role in it is not easy, and I know that. For some who look at this new world that's forming with its chaos, confusion, and complexity, the only way they can handle it is to just stay out. They huddle in bunkers, create gated churches, create a unique Christian subculture, and do search and rescue missions."10

One week you could lead a discussion on the pros and cons of Christian schools, radio, and television, versus those of public schools, secular radio, and mainstream television.

11. We have focused on external change, not internal change.

We must not try to just change people on the outside but change them on the inside as well. We know that only the Spirit of the living God can change a person. This change happens from the inside out. Remind your leaders that you are not calling them to go and impact their world and make *better* people. You are asking them to bring Jesus Christ with them to a lost secular marketplace and to allow *Him* to make them and others *new* people — different from before (see Matthew 23:27; Mark 7:21-23; 2 Corinthians 5:17). Ask your group, "What makes believers different than many good civic organizations? Should we be involved as Christians in such organizations in our communities and businesses? Why or why not?"

12. We have focused on individualism instead of teamwork.

When will we ever learn that we cannot control what the Spirit of God is doing in our neighborhoods, workplaces, or even our churches? All of us, workplace leaders and pastors alike, must realize that the best we can do is join God in what He is doing among the lost and His children who surround us every day. Peter Senge said it directly: "Give up being in control. It's hard for those of us who are immigrants, who have been taught that being in control and in charge is what it means to be a leader."[11] Ken Blanchard said, "Jesus has three years in which to save the world. What does he do? He builds a team. He shares power."[12] Ask each of your leaders which areas of their lives (for example, work, marriage, parenting, finances) they still try to control.

CONCLUSION

Helping your leaders get a vision for joining God in workplace ministry may very well mean giving them new perspectives (and likely encouraging them to give up some old ones). Take these men and women aside (just as Jesus would) and together gently confront and hurdle any obstacles that may stand in their way. As they experience a deeper life in Christ and with others, they will awaken to what God is doing around them.

ACTION STEPS

1. Have your group make a list of the traditions in your church that they feel are dead and need changing. (Make your list ahead of time and compare it with theirs.)

2. Have each of your members share one tradition or obstacle that he or she struggles with the most, and get group interaction on how to change that pattern of thinking.

3. As suggested in this chapter, spend at least one meeting discussing the fruit of the Spirit (see Galatians 5:22-23) and how we get these character qualities into our lives. Then, ask members to give an example of one fruit that God is developing in them in their workplace.

"DO NOT LET THIS BOOK
OF THE LAW
DEPART FROM
YOUR MOUTH; MEDITATE
ON IT DAY
AND NIGHT,

SO THAT YOU MAY BE
CAREFUL TO DO
EVERYTHING WRITTEN
IN IT. THEN YOU
WILL BE
PROSPEROUS
AND SUCCESSFUL."

—JOSHUA 1:8

CHAPTER V

KEY MENTORING AREAS

~~~⌒)

AS YOU MENTOR the workplace leaders of your church, two areas will emerge that are paramount to their spiritual growth. Each is difficult for leaders to acknowledge and work through, so they particularly need your guidance and accountability as they face them. These areas are (1) coping with success, and (2) giving up control to God.

COPING WITH SUCCESS

> Those who went ahead and those who followed shouted, "Hosanna!" "Blessed is he who comes in the name of the Lord!" "Blessed is the coming kingdom of our father David!" "Hosanna in the highest!" (Mark 11:9-10)

After three years of public ministry, Jesus entered Jerusalem triumphantly. Throughout His ministry Jesus had to deal with the crowds, but this day they were ready to finally crown Him as King. Though we know that the crowd's mood would change dramatically over the next few days, Jesus never let them deter Him from His ultimate purpose. The religious leaders were always there, the crowd changed from hot to cold to hot, but Jesus continued to equip the Twelve and walked steadily toward the cross. He knew that worldly success is fleeting. Each of your key leaders will probably have a good measure of success in the workplace, financially, and in other areas. How they handle these exuberant times will greatly determine how they finish the race. The following story points to the fact that although handling success is crucial to one's continued spiritual growth, people seldom give much thought or planning to it.

The young man sitting across the restaurant table from me was just under thirty years of age and had recently sold his first company for several million dollars. We were talking about business, spiritual matters, and life. I had casually made the comment that in my experience, eight out of ten men that I knew, even believers, had been harmed by business or material success. He was shocked and scoffed at the notion. As we continued our lunch, I silently prayed that God would give him wisdom and discernment.

Several weeks later I received this e-mail from him:

> Since we met, I have been pondering [what you said]. I have a few young friends who are still Christians and CEOs or presidents of their companies. As I have talked to them in recent weeks, I asked them many of the same questions that you asked me. My opinion is that every one of them is heading for one of the three big traps — the lust of the eyes, the lust of the flesh, or the pride in what

one has or does. I want to make a difference in the
lives of these men. Do you have any thoughts?

I wish that I could let you sit in on numerous conversations like
that one. More than twenty-five years ago, a dear and godly pastor
prayed for God to bless the work of three young businessmen. All
three achieved financial success. Just six years later, one of the men
had gone through a divorce, and another had experienced bankruptcy
due to unwise and frivolous spending after gaining sudden success and
wealth. Later, the preacher told me that he would never pray that way
again. Few people can stand financial prosperity. Some will be derailed
by constantly comparing themselves with others. Others will be taken
off the path when they respond wrongly to suffering. However, the
most dangerous spiritual obstacle that leaders can face is when they
have no problems and have to learn how to deal with success.

That is why you need to have their attention long before that day
arrives. As their pastor, mentor, coach, and teacher, you must warn
them of the pitfalls of prosperity, perhaps using one of your meetings
to discuss a passage such as Deuteronomy 8. Success is not evil; it just
makes it easier to focus on ourselves and to not depend on God. Most
men and women can come back from discouragement, defeat, despair,
and even depression. Few can deal with continued success, particularly
if it comes early in life.

So first, let me provide a few definitions of success. Next, we will
look at a few myths about success, and then why worldly success is so
alluring to your leaders. Finally, we will explore success as God views
it.

What Is Success?

My friend Ford Madison has said, "Success is a direction, not a destination; a process, not a project."[1] I have heard it said that success is obedience to God. Larry Burkett says, "Success is surrender to God's authority—obedience—persistence."[2] Anthony Campolo states, "The success fantasy is wealth, power, and prestige. While these are not evil, they can be destructive when abused and overemphasized."[3]

My definition of success is this: Success for the Christian is a daily process, a balanced life lived on God's terms in the power of the Holy Spirit.

The Bible tells us that ultimate success is to hear our Master say, "Well done, good and faithful servant" (Matthew 25:21). Success depends on a disposition to obey God. It is a natural result of following God's principles.

Myths of Success

There are many myths of success in the marketplace. One myth is that "bigger is better." The fact is, size does not guarantee success; in fact, the opposite is often true. The bigger you get, the harder it is to keep doing the basics well. Every business or organization has a right size. It gains efficiencies up to a certain point, and then starts to lose any size advantage. You need to know this because building a firm takes a toll on a leader. As a CEO, I had to make choices and keep certain priorities, which was hard to do when facing the huge pressures of growth.

Second, it is a myth that in order to make money, you must take advantage of others. Leaders may feel that everybody in the business is doing it, and they will be left behind if they do not follow suit. When I was a very young man learning from my Christian businessman father, I was given this philosophy: "Win/win for all" (supplier/you/customer). When a leader goes into negotiations, contracts, or relationships with this rule in mind, there is a good result for all parties.

Third, some say that you must sacrifice your family to succeed. It is very easy for a leader to become a workaholic, actually thinking that he or she has to be that way and that the leader's family must learn to understand the excessive time demand on his or her life. This is a satanic tactic for destruction of the family. If Satan can't destroy the family with direct sin such as adultery, he will push us until relationships crumble as a result of exhaustion and neglect. A leader must learn to put a limit on his or her hours. That's why he or she needs an accountability group.

A fourth myth is that the "system" is the solution and that individuals are there only to run the system. Some companies wrongly think that people are not important. Truly successful companies value the worth of every person, just as God does.

A final myth is that success requires long-term planning and luck. A true believer understands the power and sovereignty of God. Most of my problems have been due to *my mistakes*. Most of my success was due to *God's intervention*. A Christian leader must be on his or her knees daily asking God for wisdom. Every leader who is walking with God will see the handprint of God on every major opportunity.

You, as a pastor, must frankly discuss each of these myths with your leaders. You must help them avoid pitfalls.

WORLDLY SUCCESS

There are three types of worldly successes to which leaders are drawn. John warns us of these in 1 John 2:15-16. The first is *accomplishment* or acclaim. Solomon says that it provides little satisfaction (see Ecclesiastes 2:11; 3:9; 5:16). (By the way, the book of Ecclesiastes is another excellent Bible portion to study with your leaders.)

Second, we are drawn to *accumulation*. The question we must ask ourselves early and often is, "How much is enough?" This is a struggle for people who are financially successful, even if they have a heart for God. They must constantly readjust their focus. The book of Proverbs speaks much of the pitfall of riches (see Proverbs 16:8), Jeremiah warns of greed (see Jeremiah 6:13; 8:10), and Jesus asked, "What good is it for a man to gain the whole world, yet forfeit his soul?" (Mark 8:36). I encourage self-employed leaders to pray and to pick a percentage of income to give back to God before the year starts (10 percent, 15 percent, 20 percent, or 50 percent) and then rely on God and His sovereignty through each day, decision, and relationship to determine the outcome of the company for the year.

The third type of worldly success is having our *appetites* filled (see Isaiah 56:11). As Emily Dickinson wrote, "Success is counted sweetest by those who ne'er succeed." No amount of money can buy enough entertainment to satisfy our soul.

It's ideal when we can ask older leaders who have tasted from each of these three wells to testify to our young leaders that worldly success can never satisfy the longings of our heart. Considering the results of seeking worldly success, some have come to this conclusion: Success is not found primarily in the position that you hold, the possessions you obtain, or the prestige you are granted; rather, success is the person that you are.

SPIRITUAL SUCCESS

What does God's Word say about success? In Deuteronomy 30:11-16, we are told that success is not difficult to find. It is based on God's Word, worshiping God, walking with God, and obeying the will of God.

If we are to be successful leaders, we must have a thirst and respect for the Word of God (see Deuteronomy 29:9) and must daily drink of its truth (see Psalm 1:3). Next, we must focus on worshiping God. Jesus' Greatest Commandment is that we should worship God with all of our heart (see Matthew 22:37). As a leader spends time in God's Word and focuses on Him, he or she learns to have a dependent walk with God. God, rather than the person's own efforts, becomes the source of success. We see this in the life of Abraham (see Genesis 24), Joseph (see Genesis 39:2-3,23), David (see 1 Chronicles 18:6), Uzziah (see 2 Chronicles 26:5), Hezekiah (see 2 Chronicles 31:21), and Nehemiah (see Nehemiah 1:11).

Finally, as a leader walks with God, it becomes easier for him or her to make right choices and be in God's will. God is very plain in His Word about choices (see 1 Chronicles 22:13). As Psalm 25:12 promises, "Who, then, is the man that fears the LORD? He will instruct him in the way chosen for him." I particularly like verses 12 and 13 as paraphrased in *The Living Bible*. God teaches us "how to choose the best" and we "live within God's circle of blessing." Now, *that* is success!

As Ford Madison said, success is a journey, not a destination; and the result of spiritual success will be maturity and ministry to others. Jesus talked of doing God's will and finishing His work (see John 4:34). Paul said, "To live is Christ" (Philippians 1:21). James urges us to persevere (see James 1:4). May you proactively coach your leaders in this area. May they enjoy the blessings of God and the results of right decisions made early. May they use any outward trappings of worldly success as tools to draw others to a deeper relationship with Jesus Christ. Success can be used as a bridge to bring others to Him.

Teach your leaders that God does not want what they have; He wants them. If He has them, then He can use what they have. We can never obey God too completely or love Him too much. Patrick Morley says, "With Christ, success is not performance; it is surrender. To succeed is to surrender your motives, ambitions, and priorities to Christ."4

Humility and surrender of control are not characteristics that come easily to anyone. But they are essential to becoming godly leaders and influencers in the workplace. This leads us into the second critical area for leaders to embrace: giving up control of their lives and work to God.

LEARNING TO GIVE UP CONTROL

For the sake of a biblical example and a source for study for your group, consider the life of Joseph. Joseph was a man God transformed from a spoiled kid into a leader who He used to bless others (see Genesis 37–45). As a young man, Joseph was his father's favorite, used to having his way. He taunted his brothers with the interpretations of his dreams in which he ruled over them. Eventually, he invited their hate. (Ask your leaders if they know someone like this in their work world, and it's likely they will.) But as Joseph faced crises, including slavery and false imprisonment (personal bankruptcy), he not only survived by trusting God but rose to great occasions.

You know the story and the lessons, but permit me to list them as a workplace leader might see them. Joseph learned to trust God in times of adversity and testing (see Genesis 37:18; 39:10). He came to understand that God's Spirit was with him and that others noticed it (see 39:2-3). He became a servant (see 39:4; 40:4). He learned that God might bless others on account of him (see 39:5). He remained faithful in his responsibilities (see 39:6,22). During this period, *he became dependent on God rather than remaining independent.*

Joseph did not have the written Word of God, but he must have listened to the "stories" of godly family members because he knew God's Laws (see 39:9). He was sensitive to those around him (see 40:7). (Sensitivity is one of the most difficult lessons that I have had to learn as a leader in the workplace.) Joseph learned patience as God took time to work in his life. He gave credit to God in everything during the good times (see 40:8; 41:16,25,28,32). So many times when leaders gain success they forget where it came from.

Joseph understood that we are only stewards of God's blessings and that we possess nothing of ourselves (see 41:14-16,39,41,43,45-46). He understood that God had sent him to that place for that time (see 45:7). He realized that he was only a pilgrim passing through. Business leaders must not get too attached to the things in the workplace, because this is not their permanent home. Ultimately, Joseph was convinced that God was sovereign and in control of the situation, as he explained to his brothers, now reunited with him in Egypt while famine raged in Israel: "Am I in the place of God? You intended to harm me, but God intended it for good to accomplish what is now being done, the saving of many lives" (50:19-20).

Leaders must intentionally give up control of their lives to God or He will bring about the circumstances to show them that they were never in control in the first place. Learning to give up their right to make decisions is nothing more than an outward visible sign of the inward spiritual battle that they face every day.

I understand that in the late 1980s, the prime minister of Singapore, then sixty-four, voluntarily gave up his post to a man in his forties. Despite the fact that the country was doing well, he believed that his most important task was to select the next prime minister and make sure he was qualified. Ten years later, the former leader was still in good health and able to advise. However, his successor, because of his younger age, was able to effectively deal with a changing world economy.

In the same way, God wants us to learn that voluntarily turning over our lives will reap benefits; in our case, those benefits are for eternity.

How remarkable that Jesus, the Lord of the universe, voluntarily humbled Himself (see Philippians 2:1-11). We must learn from His example and make our satisfaction in life be that we understand and know Him and His ways (see Jeremiah 9:24). As you mentor your leaders, work with them on what they depend on and focus on.

ACTION STEPS

1. Take a week or two to cover these topics thoroughly with your leaders. They hear a lot of the world's philosophy, but few have studied the biblical view.

2. Share with them some of the myths of success with which pastors struggle. Your vulnerability will allow them to share their struggles in this area.

3. Have each leader take a week to think about and write out his or her definition of success.

4. Ask the group to openly discuss the possible pitfalls of selling out to worldly success. Ask each leader which path-way tempts him or her the most.

5. Ask your group how far God will go in order to prepare a leader. Have them share examples from the Bible or from their own lives.

6. Share with the group one or two occasions when God allowed you to be broken. What were the results of these times of testing?

7. Ask your group why we tend not to grow during good times. What kinds of things can leaders do to prepare themselves for times of trial and testing?

GREET PRISCILLA AND
AQUILA, MY FELLOW
WORKERS IN
CHRIST JESUS.
THEY RISKED THEIR
LIVES FOR ME. NOT ONLY
I BUT ALL THE CHURCHES OF

THE GENTILES ARE
GRATEFUL TO THEM.
GREET ALSO THE
CHURCH
THAT MEETS AT
THEIR HOUSE.

—ROMANS 16:3-5

CHAPTER VI

CREATIVE APPROACHES TO
MINISTRY IN THE MARKETPLACE

AQUILA AND PRISCILLA were a marvelous couple and a great example of both energy and creativity in the ministry to the marketplace. Everywhere you turn, there they are, making tents and leading people to Jesus. They left Rome and moved to Corinth (see Acts 18:2), and from there we find them traveling with Paul to Syria (see18:18). Later, they show up in Ephesus, mentoring the famous evangelist Apollos (see 18:26). Paul mentions them as traveling companions when writing to the church in Corinth (see 1 Corinthians 16:19), and we see them again in Rome with a church that is meeting in their house; in fact, Paul thanks them for risking their lives to save him (see Romans 16:3-5). Finally, Paul greets them when he writes to his beloved Timothy (see 2 Timothy 4:19).

Aquila and Priscilla were key participants in spreading the gospel throughout the Mediterranean world, just as were Paul, Timothy, and Luke. Willing to move as needed to share Christ, they were obvious leaders who understood their calling and worked hard at it. Wherever God's Spirit led, they went, passionate in pursuing God and reaching others, continually looking for open doors to present the good news.

You will have some leaders who are this passionate about ministry. Although most will stay put, you will have a few who decide to move location or position as a result of God's refocusing their ministry vision. You will have a very few who are willing to risk everything for God's leading. You have the exciting job of mentoring the Aquilas and Priscillas of the twenty-first century.

Priscilla and Aquila helped coin a phrase that we still use today. Believers that are missionaries and pay their own way are called "tentmakers." They earn their own income as they minister. Sometimes we mistakenly say, "They work *so that* they can proclaim Christ." It would be more correct to say, "They work *as* they proclaim Christ." Early believers used their jobs and their homes as platforms to proclaim the gospel. We need to do the same. Have we lost the simplicity of their method?

To work *as* you proclaim Christ is to live an integrated life. In such a life there is no difference in the spirituality of Sunday at church and the spirituality of Monday at work. They are the same. It made no difference to Priscilla and Aquila whether they were traveling, inviting people into their home, or making tents; they were living a life focused on God, looking for opportunities to love people to Jesus.

It took years for me to learn this principle of integration, but it has been primary in my life since an evening many years ago. I was driving home from work, in a hurry, as usual. I had barely given myself enough time to get home, grab a quick sandwich, and get to church for an outreach activity there. But something was nagging at me. I had an uneasy feeling that I couldn't shake: *What is wrong here, God?* As I drove, the Spirit seemed to ask me why I was going to visit someone I did not know when I had not stopped to listen to the fellow at the next desk who was struggling with a teenager in trouble. That question changed my life and ministry. At the time, I was so focused on keeping a commitment to an activity that I had missed the prompting of God to be sensitive to a coworker in distress.

Do your people feel the freedom and support to engage themselves in the life of another, whenever and wherever God is working, even if it conflicts with a church activity? It takes time and spontaneity to build relationships, but that is where God wants our focus to be.

The principle of integration is important to teach your leaders and important for them to grasp. Merging the secular with the sacred and integrating faith with work is not an easy assignment. Sadly, most believers today still view evangelism as a course, an event, or an activity instead of a lifestyle of naturally exposing people to God's love.

As Deuteronomy 6:6-7 instructs, we are to proclaim God's principles *as we go.* The opportunities are limitless. Your leaders can use their actions, their ears, their eyes, and their voices. Letters, Bibles, Christian books, birthday cards, holiday greetings, simple notes, conversations over lunch, hospital visits, and offers of comfort during times of crisis become ministry tools. In my earlier book, *Show and Then Tell: Presenting the Gospel Through Daily Encounters,* I explained in detail how to recognize "open doors" of opportunity to minister. In that book, I told more than a hundred stories of ordinary people sharing Christ where they live, work, and play. In this chapter, I'll merely summarize the workplace suggestions.[1]

Some of the following examples will seem simple to the extreme, obvious to anyone. But in my experience, it is the smallest opportunity that is most easily overlooked. When one's day is already full and busy, it is easy to see opportunities as interruptions and to see people as problems. The remedy is to begin each day with a sincere prayer that God would enable us to see events and people through His eyes. If we can see beyond people's roughness to their pain, we can build relationships that God can use to draw those men and women to Himself.

BUILDING RELATIONSHIPS

Consider the following eight ways to build authentic relationships in the workplace:

1. Learn the *names* of people in your department or that you see on a regular basis at work.

2. Use accepted *questions* such as "How are things going?" and build on the responses to discover someone's interests and distinctives.

3. Recognize the *needs* people have in times of both suffering and success. There are needs to be understood and appreciated. Build on this time of openness to be a special friend.

4. Don't take *breaks* or have *lunch* alone. Invite someone to join you, but keep it casual and light.

5. Become an *interesting person* yourself. Read, listen, and watch what is going on locally, regionally, nationally, and worldwide.

6. Be alert to areas of *common interest* as you meet various people, both for networking purposes and for developing your relationships. Most of us can make conversation easily about areas in which we share an interest, be it skiing, painting, children, family roots, or new software.

7. Develop a list of people for whom you will *pray* regularly. Praying for people gives you a heart for them, and they sense your love and caring. A relationship is underway.

8. Establish and nurture such a relationship by regularly looking for ways to *serve* and *minister*. Such ministry will often occur during times of crisis (health problems, financial difficulties, issues with children and one's marriage, a friend or relative's death, stresses in the workplace). Our job as believers is to build relationships, pray, and watch for opportunities. God will be faithful in giving these open doors to your leaders if they are sensitive to His leading and available to follow it.

Once your leaders visualize the open door, they can tactfully share Christ. Equip them to be able to do that. Teach them how to share their own experiences of meeting God and living with Him. It helps if they can initially write out a three-minute version of their own personal story and practice telling it to the group. That way, they have something they can share over coffee in a nonthreatening way. You could also teach them how to use a tract, such as "Steps to Peace with God," or show them how to draw out the Bridge Illustration on a piece of paper or napkin. Prepare them to share the good news anytime, anywhere.

TARGETING THE WORKPLACE

The marketplace is a viable place for evangelism and discipleship, but both must be done tactfully in response to personal relationships. Teach your leaders to carefully consider timing when they are presented with an opportunity to share verbally. As an employer, I have had to warn believers in my company that they would be disciplined if they "cornered" coworkers while on the clock. Such timing is unfair to the coworker, who does not have the option to leave, and it is dishonest to the employer, who is paying for time spent doing the company's work.

A believer must even think twice about having a serious conversation during break time or in a company lunchroom, where other employees can see, wonder about the topic of conversation, and gossip. I have found that people will not reject a loving servant, but they may reject the gospel when presented inappropriately.

Your leaders should always be prepared with a compassionate response to a serious concern by a coworker; then, if a door opens for an evangelistic encounter, they can say something such as, "Can we talk for a few minutes after work? I have something I want to give you that has been a great help to me" (that "something" being a personal testimony, a tract, or an illustration). An opportunity to listen and counsel could be postponed by saying, "Could we meet somewhere after work? Could I take you to dinner? I really want to hear what's going on with you. I'd like to pray for you and be there for you."

A few of your leaders actually *can* use business time to talk to their coworkers; these are the CEOs and business owners, whose jobs include taking care of their employees. As a CEO, I had an "open-door" policy, meaning that any employee could ask for my time and I would give it. If the employee was male, I could talk with him behind a closed door for privacy. If the employee was female, I had another woman present whom the employee trusted, usually my wife. I asked for the employee's permission first to make sure she would be comfortable with that arrangement. On a few occasions, my wife took the woman out of the building to talk over a long lunch, or I arranged for our company chaplain to become involved. In any event, it required planning to ensure privacy, the comfort of the employee, and a legal safeguard for myself. It is sad that our society has dissolved into this state, but it has, and such a safeguard is necessary. Leaders must be "wise as serpents and yet as harmless as doves" (Matthew 10:16, PH).

Christian CEOs and business owners have unusual opportunities for spiritual influence because of their positions. Most importantly, they can set a godly example and model integrity and other values. They can lead a Bible study group before work, openly show concern, pray for others, or offer words of encouragement. Let me list other practical steps a CEO can take. These are a few of many; let your leaders add more.

The following two lists are written as if to the business leader so that you may copy them and use them with your group if you desire.

TWENTY-ONE WAYS A CEO MAY MINISTER

1. Establish written biblical values as a priority in your firm. Teach them to incoming employees. Talk about them at company meetings. Model their importance to you.

2. Provide seminars from a biblical viewpoint, free to employees and held during company time, about finances, children, marriage, and the like. An employee committee can pick the topics and speakers. Seminars should be optional to avoid "forcing" life teaching on anyone (another social and legal thorn).

3. Make available Christian books on current topics.

4. Offer to send children of your employees to a Christian camp.

5. Use Christian motivational speakers at sales or annual meetings.

6. Have a company chaplain (supplied by organizations such as Marketplace Ministries).

7. Have a prayer at company banquets.

8. Offer to send employees and their spouses to a weekend Family Life seminar (sponsored by Campus Crusade).

9. Use special seasons — such as the New Year, Thanksgiving, and Christmas — to send letters with a tactful gospel message to suppliers, customers, employees, and competitors.

10. Share your views on a current topic or personal challenge that you are facing through a monthly employee letter. (Spouses will eagerly read this one.) Make it biblically based or share a verse, but avoid "preaching" or "religious" language.

11. Make available, free to employees, one-year Bibles or a current modern Bible paraphrase, such as *The Message*. Put them on a table, perhaps at break time, and explain that they are free to anyone who would like one. Avoid using the word *gift* or referring to any holiday. That way people who, by religious preference, do not accept gifts or acknowledge holidays will still take one. I did this yearly and had up to a 75 percent response from employees.

12. Join a weekly group of fellow CEOs or business associates for encouragement and accountability. These groups are available through Fellowship of Companies for Christ,

International; Christian Businessmen's Committee; and others.

13. Offer a selection of Christian children's books to your employees. They will read these to their children and grand-children, even though they may not regularly attend a church.

14. Use part of your firm's profits to support ministries in your city, another state, or a foreign country. Freely share what God has provided.

15. Send some of your key people to a lay conference where they can relate to other business and professional leaders.

16. Lead a group of your employees in a study of Judeo-Christian values.

17. Share your profits and help your employees provide for their futures through a generous retirement plan. Teach them the value of saving, long-term investing, and compound interest.

18. Provide educational scholarships to the children of your employees. Let them know that families are a priority to you.

19. Share your values with key suppliers; maybe send them *The Message* book of Proverbs. Add a note saying, "This is a great book of business principles." Pay them on time so that you will have a positive testimony to them.

20. Examine your overtime hours and travel schedules to make sure your family remains a priority, regardless of competitive pressures.

21. Become a servant. Give up your reserved parking space.

MINISTERING IN THE MARKETPLACE

Obviously, most workplace leaders are not CEOs and owners. The following list of ideas can be used by *anyone* to minister in the marketplace.

* *Care* — Use lunches as a time to build relationships with fellow employees and business associates.

* *Encouragement* — Send birthday or anniversary cards to fellow associates. They could have a Christian message or verse. Add a short handwritten message, and sign them. Most adults do not receive cards from anyone other than immediate family members. They will be surprised and

appreciative.

* *Comfort* — Use times of crisis (illness, divorce, death, and so on) to share the comfort of Christ. Send a card. Visit a hospital.

* *Hospitality* — Invite fellow workers to your home for recreation, dinner, and fellowship. Take them to a sporting event.

* *Fellowship* — Lead a group Bible study before work or over lunch.

* *Thanksgiving* — Use simple thank-you notes to show appreciation to another person for specific acts. Fewer than 10 percent of the people they encounter ever say "thank you."

* *Joy* — Be positive, use clean language, and don't allow yourself to be a part of any negative, critical, or judgmental talk. Be a bridge builder. Share times of joy at births, marriages, or graduations.

* *Patience* — Ask God to give you a special spirit to deal with times of crisis and pressure. Others will see the difference in your life.

* *Concern* — Listen to a friend who is having difficulties with a child. Loan that person a book about raising children, discipline, or whatever you think might be appropriate.

* *Evangelism* — Let your supervisor, vendors, customers, and fellow associates know that you practice biblical principles in the marketplace. This gives an opening to share your faith.

* *Prayer* — Offer to pray for an associate who shares a problem with you. Put it on a 3 x 5 card to remind yourself. Pray for the person as you exercise, walk, or drive. Check back in a few days or weeks for an update.

* *Travel* — When traveling with associates, you have great opportunities (in a car, at an airport, in a restaurant) to talk about important things in life.

* *Listening* — Listen first to the Holy Spirit for guidance and then to the people around you.

Each leader needs to pattern the activity after his or her personality and gifting. It will take months, even years, to refine the process. But with your help as mentor and encourager, these leaders will be able to dramatically impact those around them. After some practice, anyone can become proficient at allowing the light of the living Christ to shine through. Each one can truly be "unashamed of the gospel."

SOWING SEEDS

What does it look like to minister in the world every day? Lorne Sanny, former longtime president of The Navigators and a humble leader, is now in his eighties and battling cancer. Yet, he writes of his persistence to "sow seeds."

In my personal life I'm a seed sower. I try, wherever I am, every day, to sow a seed of the Word. Most of the time it seems to fall on hard, rocky, or thorny ground. Occasionally it falls on good ground. As little as I seem to be reaping, I'm committed to keep on sowing, every day.

Just the other day, in the mall, I told an inquiring clerk that I was waiting for my wife. I asked him if he was married. He replied, "Yes, three times and divorced three times." My comment: "That must be extremely painful. Do you ever ask for help from 'upstairs'?" He said, "Yes, I do." I added a sentence or two and left the store. It took less than five minutes, but I think I sowed a tiny seed.[2]

Do your leaders use their workplace platforms to minister to the needs of others and verbally share Christ with them as God gives opportunity? Sit down with your leaders and strategize with them as if they were missionaries in a pagan land, because they are.

ACTION STEPS

1. Go around the circle and ask everyone to pick one day from the previous week and share examples of how they integrated their secular and spiritual lives.

2. Ask your leaders to memorize Deuteronomy 6:6-7. Meditate on the verses for a week. Ask them, "What does this look like in your life?"

3. Have your leaders tell about an experience that they had sharing Christ in the workplace.

4. Teach your leaders two or three ways they can share Christ (testimony, tract, diagram such as the Bridge). Have them practice with each other.

THEN JESUS
SAID TO THEM,
"GIVE TO CAESAR
WHAT IS
CAESAR'S
AND TO GOD

WHAT IS GOD'S."
AND THEY
WERE
AMAZED AT HIM.

—MARK 12:17

CHAPTER VII

MODELING THE MESSAGE IN A SECULAR CULTURE

IN THE VERSE quoted on the left, Jesus emphasized that each of us is to center on God with all of our heart and yet still meet the obligations of this world's system. We must live our life with one eye focused on eternity and the other focused on our temporal situation. Daily, each one of your leaders struggles with a fully integrated life. Of the many biblical examples of this issue, the one I like best is Daniel, who not only survived but also thrived in a secular culture while keeping his focus on God. You know the story well, but let's revisit it for a few minutes.

ALIEN IN A FOREIGN LAND

Exiled from his home in Jerusalem as a young teenager, Daniel nonetheless proved his faithfulness to God in Babylon's changing political environment. He served four different kings during the period of Israel's seventy-year captivity and was a consistent godly influence in a pagan culture.

How was a man of such character and spiritual consistency

developed in a place lacking the influence or support of family or temple? He had obviously made a fierce commitment to God, a fact that was immediately and radically revealed when he refused to eat meat that had been offered to idols. He fed this commitment with the daily habit of entering God's presence in prayer. Daniel understood God's wisdom, sovereignty, holiness, and faithfulness — and his courage was the result of his unwavering belief (see Daniel 2; 5).

Move ahead in the story to Daniel 6. Daniel, now about eighty years old, had become one of the three vice presidents of the land and was in line for promotion. His adversaries, in their effort to discredit him to the king, could find only Daniel's dependence upon God as a "weakness," so they tricked the king into signing a decree that forbid praying to any gods other than the king himself. Yet, what did Daniel do? "Now when Daniel learned that the decree had been published, he went home to his upstairs room where the windows opened toward Jerusalem. Three times a day he got down on his knees and prayed, giving thanks to his God, just as he had done before" (Daniel 6:10). He did not change the pattern to which he had committed himself decades before. As you know, God delivered Daniel from death in the lions' den and secured his promotion in the kingdom as well.

Today we need men and women like Daniel. Richard Halverson writes,

> In what way does the church have its maximum impact on the world? What is its greatest influ-

ence? . . . The follower of Jesus Christ must be prepared with certain equipment and basics if he
expects to be effective. . . . His preparation is in private devotions, public worship, Bible reading and
study, memorizing, and most of all, disciplining himself in his step by step, moment by moment relationship with Jesus Christ. To be precise, the real
influence of the believer in the world is not what he
does for Christ. . . . It is the life of Christ working in
and through the believer! (see Galatians 2:20). . . . The
authentic impact of the believer in the world is righteousness! . . . Activism apart from righteousness
(Christlikeness) is infinitely less than the authentic
influence of the believer in the world! "You are the
salt of the earth" (Matthew 5:13).[1]

There are several reasons why we, as the body of Christ, are not
having a greater impact in our world today. First, the lives of believers in the church are sometimes not much different from their
unbelieving friends. Second, some Christians have purposely separated from the culture and have most of their connections with the
Christian subculture. This is not necessarily bad on all counts, but
it does segment us. The workplace is one of the few places that these
Christians find unbelieving friends (assuming, of course, that they
don't work for a Christian organization). Finally, most of those who
are engaged in the culture do not understand its influence and how
they are affected by it; therefore, most believers are not as effective

change agents as they could be. May we all, pastors and workplace leaders alike, resolve to be more Daniel-like with our each and every culture contact.

INFLUENCING OUR CULTURE

Let's look at some of the lessons that we may learn from Daniel's example and to which the leaders in your group should give some thought if they haven't already. Obviously, the culture around us is far from neutral — it is out to change the way we think, act, and live. We should be careful not to violate our beliefs in adapting to the culture. We must, like Daniel, propose creative alternatives to our employers, customers, and coworkers when confronted with unChristian expectations of us. We need to understand that God will provide everything that we need to survive in the culture. As we face challenges, we need to ask God to give us discretion and discernment and to praise Him privately and publicly when He provides for us. He, not the culture, is to be our focus. Notice that when talking to his superiors, Daniel gave God the credit (see Daniel 1–2).

Daniel's story shows that those in authority *will* notice a godly life. In engaging with the culture, God may allow us to serve under numerous superiors or administrators. Some may be easier to work for than others. Regardless, we must endure change and allow God to use it to mold us. Others in our sphere of influence may become jealous of us if God allows us to be promoted or be successful. However, we must never neglect spiritual input, regardless of the cost. God places leaders in various businesses or cultures to be living models for Christ. Even in our most difficult circumstances, we must remember that God is in control; He is sovereign, and He may choose to deliver us, but if not, He still has an eternal plan for our lives.

It is very important to God how we behave among those who are outside the faith.

Paul wrote, "The overseer . . . must also have a good reputation with outsiders" (1 Timothy 3:2,7) and also, "that your daily life may win the respect of outsiders" (1 Thessalonians 4:12). I love how Eugene Peterson paraphrased Colossians 4:5-6 in *The Message:* "Use your heads as you *live* and *work* among *outsiders*. Don't miss a trick. Make the most of every opportunity. Be gracious in your speech. The goal is to bring out the *best* in others in a conversation, not put them down, not cut them out" (emphasis added).

Consider the following real-life stories of Christian leaders in their workplaces who are taking opportunities daily to influence those around them for Christ. One is a lawyer, one is a supervisor, another is a salesman, and the last is a schoolteacher. I could have chosen any number of people from any number of fields, but these will give a sampling, food for thought, as you and your group explore ways in which God uses leaders in the marketplace.

INFLUENCING OUR LEGAL SYSTEM

John Burris was a Tulsa attorney working for the state of Oklahoma. He often had a chance to share the Scriptures with a particular judge. This judge had attended church as a child, but she was not a believer. Months passed as John continued to share his faith. One day the judge called to say that she had been asked to transfer away from Tulsa to a place where her husband had an established practice and where they had a ranch close by. She was brokenhearted to think of moving.

John stated that only God could give her peace in this challenging situation and that it was time she gave her life to Christ. God's Spirit worked in her life, and she did just that over the phone with John that day. God later provided the opportunity for her to work part-time so that she did not have to move. The judge and her husband are now active in their church and their walk with Christ. Even in the legal justice arena, God is using believers to impact lives in a secular world.

INFLUENCING OUR MARKETPLACE

For many years I had an employee named Bill. When he was diagnosed with cancer, the insurance company wanted to drop his health coverage, but Bill's route supervisor, Lance, asked that we keep Bill on the payroll during his extended illness. We decided to do that. Years after his dad's death, Bill's son wrote to thank us for the financial, emotional, and spiritual encouragement we were able to provide during that time. We still minister to Bill's wife, who is in our ministry to widows. Can just one person make an eternal influence in his job? Certainly!

Wayne came to our firm through an acquisition. During the transition, Wayne lost his job supervising a facility and began to drive a van and service retail stores. As the months and years went by, he saw that God had placed him there to be a minister to his coworkers and customers. He boldly challenged his coworkers to live as Jesus Christ would in their company. In one e-mail to his coworkers, he wrote, "Every day I pray for wisdom, patience, and understanding as I deal with my customers. . . . I want to cheer them up, be courteous, and help them in some small way. . . . We need to rededicate ourselves this Easter season to be the Christians that we are." His service to Christ never wavered.

INFLUENCING OUR SCHOOL CHILDREN

Perhaps the most culturally challenging environment is our public school system. Marilyn is a Christian schoolteacher who seeks to make a difference every day in an education system in which values have been removed. She shares this story of how impacting one life can make a difference:

> It was a day my fourth-grade students had antici-pated with much excitement; we were having tryouts for parts in the Christmas musical. I had written all of the available parts on the chalkboard. Students were instructed that when I called their name, they could choose one part for which they would like to audition. They were aware I was listening for expres-sion and projection.
>
> I began at the first of the alphabet. In turn, each student who wished to audition came to the front of the classroom and read the highlighted part for which he or she wished to be considered. The students were

instructed to be polite, good listeners, and encouragers as each student tried out. I routinely continued calling the next student. Then, I reached Alice's name. Should I call her name or skip over it? I wasn't sure what to do.

Alice was mainstreamed into the fourth-grade music class from her homeroom class for emotionally disturbed students. She had never spoken in class; she walked in the hallways with her head down, never answering a "Hi, Alice!" In class, we heard only screams if she dropped her tiny toy, which always occupied her attention. Once, when asked to sit [in her assigned spot], she kicked me in the chest. No one was really sure exactly what Alice's diagnosis was, but most felt it was some sort of autism.

Time was fleeting, and I didn't have long to ponder whether or not to call on her. I said, "Alice Jones." She got up from her seat and walked to my desk. One could have heard a pin drop in the room. The students were as shocked as I. "Alice, what part would you like to try out for?" "Reindeer," she blurted out. There actually was not a speaking part for a reindeer, but she took the book, walked in front of the class, and began to read, mumbling. When she finished, the class erupted into loud clapping and cheers, and a broad smile covered Alice's face. I could hardly manage the tears that were trying to flood my eyes. What we were doing had reached her. I could hardly wait to tell her teacher when class was over. "This is why I teach," I said. A difference like this may come along only once in a whole teaching career, but it makes it all worth it.

Oh yes, Alice was a reindeer in the play! She wore her headband reindeer antlers for months. She spoke no line in the play, but danced with the other reindeer and showed no signs of stage fright. Another Christmas miracle!

Marilyn, John, Lance, and Wayne all share one thing in common. Each of them is trying to present Christ where he or she works each day. You have been given the responsibility of helping your leaders to be changed by the living Christ in order to become salt and light in the culture. What an awesome task!

ACTION STEPS

1. Ask your leaders to discuss specific ways that we can engage the culture without being polluted by it. Have them give examples of times when expectations of their behavior contradicted Christian values. Have them suggest satisfactory compromises that could be used in future situations.

2. Have your group members suggest several ways they can strengthen themselves spiritually before they engage the culture.

3. Discuss specific ways that Daniel was able to gain promotion without violating his values. How did Daniel get along with his superiors? His peers?

4. Ask group members to list three or four of the most difficult people that they deal with in the marketplace. Then have them list a current need that each of these people has as well as a strategy to meet that need.

AND THE THINGS
YOU HAVE HEARD ME
SAY IN THE
PRESENCE
OF MANY WITNESSES
ENTRUST TO

RELIABLE
MEN WHO
WILL ALSO BE QUALIFIED
TO TEACH
OTHERS.

—2 TIMOTHY 2:2

CHAPTER VIII

THE CHALLENGE TO REPRODUCE

AS A PASTOR, you want to prepare your leaders, but they must eventually be qualified to reproduce these spiritual truths in others. When we look at Jesus' plan of ministry, we know that He did not leave an organization or a building as His legacy. He left twelve men whom He taught and prepared to influence the lives of others into His kingdom. There was no other plan. He knew that unless those men reproduced, He had only reached one generation.

The same holds true now. As you release your leaders into their workplaces, you first want them to establish long-term balanced priorities. Then you want them to make eternal investments while working in a temporal, secular workplace. They must be reminded that these investments in people should be focused on the next generation. Just as you have equipped them to be reproducers, they must equip their circles of influence to reproduce in another spiritual generation.

In this chapter I'd like to focus on Jesus' intercessory prayer for the disciples, recorded in John 17 and reprinted for your convenience on pages 140 and 141. In this prayer, Jesus gave us numerous principles about this ministry of reproduction. May I encourage you to study it with your workplace leaders and let them see how they can reproduce their faith through others?

JESUS' PRAYER FOR HIS LEADERS

Let us look at just a few of the principles given in Jesus' prayer.

♦ Notice in verse 3 that our *desire* should be that everyone we work with would know Christ and experience eternal life in Him. Observe in verse 6 that we *do not have to search* for those to whom we are to minister. God is the One who gives them to us. I try to be constantly alert in each encounter to discern how God wants me to touch that life. Notice that Jesus repeated this principle in verses 9 and 24. God is sovereign and all-knowing in determining which individuals our lives are to touch. He may go to great lengths over a great time or distance to bring two lives together.

♦ Next, understand the principle given in verses 7 and 10. Everything we have comes from God. *We must be totally dependent on Him.* We must constantly remember that He is the provider and source of all that we are and have.

♦ In verse 8, we are reminded again that we must *give God's Word* to our people. Wisdom from other great leaders is good, but truth comes from the Bible. We can only give out God's Word to others as we have received it from the Father and His Spirit. This principle is repeated in verses 14 and 17. Whenever we work with other leaders, we must constantly expose them to God's Word. I do this by encouraging their devotional time and their involvement in personal Bible study, and through strong verbal messages (CDs), and written teachings (books) by skilled men and women of God.

- In verse 9, Jesus reminds us of another key principle: Every person that God gives us is "on loan" for a brief period of time. *They are not our leaders but God's.* We will not be their only mentor or coach. Our objective in raising up leaders is not success, fame, power, prestige, or building a large institution. We are to glorify Christ and lift Him up (see verse 10).

- In verses 11 and 21-23, Jesus emphasizes that we, as His followers, are to walk in *unity.* Your leaders must keep a kingdom mentality and not let divisiveness among churches or Christian groups harm the unity among the believers in their firm or industry. When two believers pray for an unsaved coworker or family in need, they do not worry about the name on the sign of the church where they worshiped on Sunday. When they are involved in spiritual warfare, they need to keep the objective in mind and know their fellow soldiers.

- In verse 12, Jesus cautions us to guard or *protect those who are less mature.* We must provide coaches, mentors, trainers, encouragers, and influencers to the marketplace so that the fruit of evangelism will not be lost. Jesus warns that we should pray for the protection of these from the enemy (see verse 15). He reminds us that we are just pilgrims passing through this world, and we are not to get attached to it (see verse 16).

- The *objective of our lives is to be holy,* which honors and glorifies Christ (see verses 17 and 19). Each leader is sent out into the world as a personal representative of Jesus Christ (see verse 18).

- Jesus did not *pray for* His disciples only but for all *future generations* that believe in Him (see verse 20). Each leader with whom you work

JESUS' PRAYER FOR HIS DISCIPLES
AND FOR ALL BELIEVERS

After Jesus said this, he looked toward heaven and prayed:

"Father, the time has come. Glorify your Son, that your Son may glorify you. ²For you granted him authority over all people that he might give eternal life to all those you have given him. ³Now this is eternal life: that they may know you, the only true God, and Jesus Christ, whom you have sent. ⁴I have brought you glory on earth by completing the work you gave me to do. ⁵And now, Father, glorify me in your presence with the glory I had with you before the world began.

⁶"I have revealed you to those you gave me out of the world. They were yours; you gave them to me and they have obeyed your word. ⁷Now they know that everything you have given me comes from you. ⁸For I gave them the words you gave me and they accepted them. They knew with certainty that I came from you, and they believed that you sent me. ⁹I pray for them. I am not praying for the world, but for those you have given me, for they are yours. ¹⁰All I have is yours, and all you have is mine. And glory has come to me through them. ¹¹I will remain in the world no longer, but they are still in the world, and I am coming to you. Holy Father, protect them by the power of your name — the name you gave me — so that they may be one as we are one. ¹²While I was with them, I protected them and kept them safe by that name you gave me. None has been lost except the one doomed to destruction so that Scripture would be fulfilled.

¹³"I am coming to you now, but I say these things while I am still in the world, so that they may have the full measure of my joy within them. [14]I have given them your word and the world has hated them, for they are not of the world any more than I am of the world. [15]My prayer is not that you take them out of the world but that you protect them from the evil one. [16]They are not of the world, even as I am not of it. [17]Sanctify them by the truth; your word is truth. [18]As you sent me into the world, I have sent them into the world. [19]For them I sanctify myself, that they too may be truly sanctified.

[20]"My prayer is not for them alone. I pray also for those who will believe in me through their message, [21]that all of them may be one, Father, just as you are in me and I am in you. May they also be in us so that the world may believe that you have sent me. [22]I have given them the glory that you gave me, that they may be one as we are one. [23]I in them and you in me. May they be brought to complete unity to let the world know that you sent me and have loved them even as you have loved me.

[24]"Father, I want those you have given me to be with me where I am, and to see my glory, the glory you have given me because you loved me before the creation of the world.

[25]"Righteous Father, though the world does not know you, I know you, and they know that you have sent me. [26]I have made you known to them, and will continue to make you known in order that the love you have for me may be in them and that I myself may be in them."

— JOHN 17:1-26

can impact multiple generations through those whom he or she touches in his or her sphere of influence. Jesus ordained this principle.

For example, I presently have a small start-up business, and I can touch the young business executive who is the son of a long-term friend as I meet with him over lunch or in a Bible study. I can mentor my business partner and coach our young VP of sales. I can influence a new employee by my actions and encouragement. I no longer have hundreds of employees scattered across the country, but my sphere of influence is still growing. I have relationships in our firm, with bankers and other investors, with accountants and attorneys, with fellow board members, and with countless entrepreneurs.

Each leader has a family, coworkers or peers, clients or customers, employers and/or employees, an extended family, vendors, and work associates. Each leader has an immediate impact group of twelve to forty and an extended group of hundreds or even thousands. Each leader is not responsible for the entire world, but he or she *is* responsible to reach his or her sphere of influence and continue the work that Jesus' disciples inherited two thousand years ago.

◆ Jesus shows us that *as we allow God to live in us* (see verse 23), *the world will understand that Christ loves them.* Isn't it amazing that God has chosen to use weak clay vessels in the workplace to show forth His light to a world in darkness? Just as God sent Christ to our world (see verse 25), Christ has commissioned each of us to the lost in our workplace.

◆ As we minister to others, we must do so *only in the power of the love of God,* which indwells us (see verse 26). We are able to give to others only as we are able to receive from God's grace.

Just as Christ prayed to the Father, you must pray to Him for your people. They in turn must pray to the Father for the followers and leaders that God has given into their care. Your leaders must model Christ's love to these as they point them to Christ.

By the way, another passage you will find helpful to discuss in your group is the entire book of 1 Thessalonians. I have found well over thirty principles in this book that we can use in our ministry of helping and equipping others. May Jesus impress upon each of us the importance of training not only followers but also reproducers.

RELEASING YOUR LEADERS

The disciples must have felt as though they were floundering when Jesus ascended to heaven. Now that He was no longer with them in the flesh every day, it was probably a nervous, and maybe even fearful, time. Jesus knew they were ready, but experience had not yet proved it to them. Still, they knew they could depend on what they had seen Him do, the things He had taught them, and the guidance of the Spirit that He had recently sent. His model was their greatest comfort.

Your leaders, too, will experience much the same as you release them to duplicate this process in their own relationships. You have been with them regularly for a long time. Now you will begin a new group, and they will reproduce what you have taught them. They are now the mentors, the teachers. Jesus' model will again provide comfort. Help them to understand it before you release them.

JESUS' MODEL

Jesus often taught in the temple or out in the countryside to *large groups* of people. This is the first environment in which we learn — large groups; it is the primary way that people are taught in our churches. Jesus modeled that method, particularly during the early years of His public ministry. Over 20 percent of the verses in the first half of Mark's gospel depict Jesus preaching or teaching in crowds.

Jesus often took aside *the Twelve*. In the first half of Mark's gospel, about 22 percent of the verses show Jesus alone with the Twelve. In the last half, this percentage more than doubles. It is not surprising that Jesus would spend His final hours with the Twelve, not the crowd.

In Mark 14:33, Jesus demonstrated yet another style — He took *three* of the disciples (Peter, James, and John) and shared privately with them. This was His *inner circle*, in whom He invested more time than He did with the other nine disciples. Many of His most trying moments were with these men. In fact, Peter would deny Him three times. Jesus obviously believed that this intimate method of influence was worth the time, and even Peter proved this to be true when he became the vibrant leader of the first-century church.

Finally, notice that in Mark 14:35, Jesus left the three and fell on His face before His Father. That Jesus would often leave the disciples to *spend time with God the Father* in prayer is recorded often in the Gospel accounts.

These four different environments — the large group, the small group, the inner circle, and time alone with God — are just as crucial for leaders to grow spiritually today. Let's consider these in a bit more detail.

ENVIRONMENTS FOR GROWTH

Each leader needs to be in a large group to worship every week. Each needs to be in a regular small group for accountability and encouragement. (This could be a small group Bible study.) This is particularly true of workplace leaders because they tend to be loners. All of us definitely need to have an inner circle. Pastors have fewer close friends than anyone. That is dangerous. As a pastor, you must pay the price and establish these key relationships. Finally, personal time with God is not an option, but a necessity for survival.

Of the four necessary environments for a healthy spiritual life, your leaders have experienced three of them during their time with you. They have participated in corporate worship at church, the environment in which you originally found them. You have helped them establish their own personal time with God throughout this period, and your group time with them has perhaps been their first experience in a small accountability group. They now know how important and helpful all three of these areas are to them. However, the fourth environment, the inner circle, might still be a mystery. This one needs to be explored before sending them out.

GOD   DEVOTIONAL LIFE

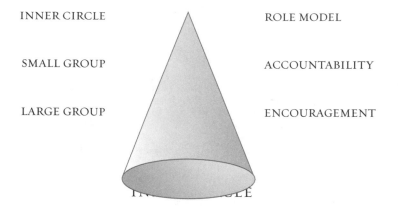

INNER CIRCLE   ROLE MODEL

SMALL GROUP   ACCOUNTABILITY

LARGE GROUP   ENCOURAGEMENT

Every person needs two or three people who care about his or her soul. When adversities and trials come, everyone needs someone who will hang on for dear life. We probably won't meet with them together as a group. Some in our inner circle may even live in a different town. But sometime in the past, we got close to them, and they still care for us like a brother or sister. While I went through several tough times, my wife and two businessmen became my inner circle. I met, cried, talked, and prayed for hours with each of them. They were indispensable. Do you have two or three people who really care about your soul? Intimacy is greatly needed today among workplace leaders as well as pastors.

In the workplace, the higher the leader's position, the more difficult it is for him or her to have close friends. Having been a CEO and business owner for thirty years, I can tell you that at times it can be a very lonely place. From talking to my pastor friends, I know this is true for them as well. God never intended for it to be this way. Therefore, Jesus modeled more than just the fellowship of the small group; He also modeled the intimate and the deep friendships of the inner circle.

I believe that Jesus wants all of us as leaders to work very hard at establishing intimacy. God does not want us to be "lone rangers." In fact, throughout Scripture He gives us examples of men and women who had close companions even as they experienced the pressure of leadership. Consider Moses and Joshua and Caleb; David and Jonathan; Elijah and Elisha; Paul and Barnabus; Paul and Timothy; Jesus and Mary, Martha, and Lazarus; Ruth and Naomi; and Daniel with his three friends, Shadrach, Meshach, and Abednego. God ordained friendship to give us needed encouragement, accountability, advice, and help in time of need.

Interestingly, the areas in which your leader is most likely to influence and reproduce are also the areas from which his or her inner circle will probably emerge. It is within these areas that relationships and strong ties need to be developed.

FAMILY

Hopefully it is true both of leaders and pastors, assuming they are married, that one member of their inner circle is their spouse. For those who have not before bared their innermost thoughts and feelings to their spouse, this will take some courage to learn. Encourage them to start with "baby steps," first sharing feelings about smaller events in life. The leader should tell his or her spouse that sharing intimately is the goal — that he or she is trying to reach out emotionally and on a heart level and would like the spouse to reciprocate. Although the spouse may initially act surprised or wary, he or she will rarely refuse such an opportunity for honest, deeper-level communication. Because society, the marketplace, and even the church at times have torn the family apart by placing too much of a time demand on the individual, every leader needs to continually develop this relationship with his or her spouse.

A leader must work to develop his or her relationship with other family members and extended family as well. Strong leaders are products, in most cases, of a strong, supportive family. In addition to his or her spouse, a leader must work to maintain relationships with grown children, parents, brothers, sisters, and grandparents. This takes planned times as a group and as individuals. Encourage your leaders to allow their families to be their number-one area of ministry.

My son and one son-in-law are pastors, so we often get together for times of mutual encouragement. My other son-in-law is a dentist and wants to live for Christ in that profession. Our two daughters and daughter-in-law are all young mothers. My wife, Davidene, is a wonderful grandmother and works hard to plan one-on-one time with the three young mothers. She also takes the grandchildren one or two at a time. This is a big commitment but is her highest spiritual priority. As a pastor, you should encourage these times from the pulpit and in your small group.

TEAMMATES IN THE MARKETPLACE *(Inside the Daily Workplace)*
Encourage your leaders to be vulnerable and available with the members of their leadership team. Outside the family, their team (not the church) is their primary area of spiritual ministry because that is where they spend the most time. Leaders need to minister to

their coworkers personally and to their coworkers' families. What a responsibility and privilege that is. For those leaders who work for a boss or a board, they must also minister to and serve them.

PEER RELATIONSHIPS (Outside the Daily Workplace)

You must encourage your leaders to work at establishing deep relationships with peers. The most helpful and encouraging times that I have had with peers were with two different groups. One was with five competitors (all Jewish) in the importing business that I met with several times a year for more than fifteen years. The dinners with these men and their spouses and informal times of sharing in the afternoons were invaluable. Each one became a dear friend over time, and God gave me frequent opportunities to minister to and share with them and their families.

My second memorable peer connection was with a group of ten other CEOs who met for a full day once a month. In the morning we had a guest speaker; in the afternoon we became a board of advisors for each other to confidentially handle key issues. We also met once a month with a paid moderator for accountability. It is interesting that although this was a secular organization, several guys came to Christ and others returned to walking with Him during my time in the group. I greatly needed the fellowship of the other CEOs! Eighty percent of our problems were the same, even though we were in ten different industries. Get your leaders into a peer group of some kind. There are now some biblically-based CEO groups sponsored by such organizations as FCCI (Fellowship of Companies for Christ International) and CBMC (formerly

Christian Businessmen's Committee but now Connecting Business and the Marketplace to Christ).

PASTORS AND THE INNER CIRCLE

Please permit me an aside at this point. I think that you, as a pastor, struggle in this area just as much as workplace leaders do. For many years pastors were told that they should not become close to the members in their churches. Thankfully, this is rapidly changing. Fifty-seven percent of our surveyed pastors have two or three close friends in their church, 27 percent have two or three close friends outside of their church, and about 16 percent have a close friend both inside and outside their church. Do whatever it takes to develop these close, confidential relationships, and then make them as regular a part of your schedule as preparing the Sunday sermon.

It is my belief that the progress the leader makes in the area of intimate, close personal relationships may ultimately determine the effectiveness of his or her leadership. As this group disperses, encourage them to keep their friendships within the group active. It may be that some relationships that have begun as a result of this ministry will become inner-circle relationships.

ACTION STEPS

1. Take time to share with your group about two or three other leaders who are mentors or current inner-circle encouragers to you.

2. Ask each member to share about one person who has impacted his or her life, spiritually or in some other way.

3. Ask leaders to share one crisis experience when they needed someone to care for their soul. Ask for volunteers to share about a time when they desperately needed someone for support but felt alone and did not ask anyone to help.

4. Encourage members of the group to meet in pairs at breakfast or lunch or spend other time together. These casual times together could lead to long-term friendships.

WE DO NOT DARE
TO CLASSIFY
OR COMPARE
OURSELVES WITH
SOME WHO COMMEND
THEMSELVES.
WHEN THEY MEASURE

THEMSELVES BY THEMSELVES
AND COMPARE
THEMSELVES WITH
THEMSELVES, THEY ARE
NOT WISE.

—2 CORINTHIANS 10:12

CHAPTER IX

TWO WARNINGS

~~~◞

AS YOU SEND out your leaders into their world, warn them about two things that can derail them: comparing themselves to others and losing sight of eternity.

WARNING #1: AVOIDING COMPARISON

There is no question that the greatest impact on one's life is probably the example of another person or persons. I have had such people in my life. Although their modeling positively affected me and I will be forever grateful, I realize that I am to focus not on them but on Jesus, who is their source of strength. We must pattern our lives after the godly character traits of others, not after their gifts, talents, or personalities. If we try to copy the uniqueness that God has graciously given them, we constantly will be disappointed. I did not learn this lesson easily.

In my mid-twenties, I spent time with three other peers who were being helped by the same mentor as I. One man had a gift for leadership and motivation; people immediately followed him because of the strength of his personality. Another discipled men regularly and still seemed to have time for others throughout his workday. A third man, gifted by God with creativity and boldness, shared his faith daily, leading many to a personal relationship with the Savior. I was frustrated because each had walked with Christ for a shorter time than I. I longed to be used by God like they were being used. It was only after I took my eyes off of them and looked to Christ Himself that God was able to begin to mold me into the young husband, father, business owner, and Christ follower He wanted me to become.

If you are honest, then you, too, probably have compared yourself to a successful minister in your early years. You were likely frustrated when things did not go as easily or quickly for you as it did for others.

God only makes originals. Teach your leaders to look for models in God's Word and not try to duplicate the work of God in others. Help them develop their God-given uniqueness. They must have freedom to use and experiment with the personality, talents, spiritual gifts, and circumstances that the sovereign God has given them. We must understand that God will use various personality types in totally different ways to minister to others. This may be a good time to do a study with them on personality types (look for books authored by experts on the subject. I recommend those by Tim LaHaye or Florence Littauer). Consider following that study with one on spiritual gifts, the understanding of which is related and essential to their God-given ministry. This will make them feel comfortable and valued doing the work and ministry that God has given them to do. It will also make them more tolerant and accepting of those whose gifting and personalities are different from their own and eliminate the discontent and frustration that comes from comparison.

When I speak in conferences, CEOs frequently ask me about the ways that we have ministered to our employees. In such cases, I do give some examples but am quick to point out that different Christian CEOs will handle the same workplace situation in vastly different ways. I am a choleric, high-"D" (driven) business owner gifted in leadership. A sensitive sanguine sales executive with a gift of mercy will minister in a totally different way. As a pastor, you must help your leaders take their eyes off of you and other visible marketplace Christians. Get them to understand themselves. What things do they do well? What goals are they passionate about? What types of ministry have they done that God has blessed and people have responded to? What do their closest friends see as their contribution to the body of Christ? As you coach these men and women, you can help them release these gifts to be used in the lives of others around them.

A cookie-cutter approach, used in so many churches, will not work. This approach to individual mentoring is often difficult, time consuming, and emotionally exhausting. However, you are training and equipping leaders who will impact hundreds and thousands of others; you dare not take shortcuts.

BECOMING LIKE CHRIST

Let me share a passage from the writings of G. D. Watson in Living Words, adapted by my friend Michael Gott. May these words speak to each of our hearts as we continually try to shift our focus off of others and onto Christ.

> Because God has called you to be really like Jesus, He will draw you into a life of crucifixion and humility and put upon you such demands of obedience that you will not be able to follow other people as a role model or measure yourself by others who serve the Lord, and in many ways He will seem to let other good people do things that He will not let you do. Be prepared for this!
>
> Other Christians and ministers who seem very authentic and effective may skillfully use secular promotional methods, push themselves forward, manipulate, and use contacts to carry out their agenda, but you cannot do it; if you attempt it, you will meet with such failure and rebuke from the Lord as to make you totally miserable.
>
> Others may congratulate themselves for their ministry and results, for their great success, and for their writings, but the Holy Spirit will not allow you to do any similar thing, and if you begin it, He will lead you into such a deep sense of guilt that will make you despise yourself and all that you have done.
>
> The Lord may let others be honored, advanced, and forged ahead. He may choose to keep you hidden in obscurity because He wants you to produce some

choice, fragrant fruit for His future glory, which can only be produced in the shade and out of sight. Be prepared; God may let others be recognized but decide to keep you overlooked. He may let others do a work for Him and get the credit for the work that you have done and thus make your reward ten times greater when Jesus comes to recognize His servants.

Settle it forever, then, that you are to deal directly with the Holy Spirit and that He is to have the privilege of tying your tongue, or chaining your hands, or closing your eyes, in ways that He does not seem to do with others. But when you are so possessed with the living God that you are, in your secret heart, pleased and delighted over this peculiar, personal, private, jealous guardianship and management of the Holy Spirit over your life, you will have found the vestibule of Heaven![1]

These are thought-provoking statements. We must, indeed, examine our motives and commit ourselves to God's sovereignty and control. I believe that is what God meant when He inspired Paul to write,

"But who are you, O man, to talk back to God? Shall what is formed say to him who formed it, 'Why did you make me like this?' Does not the potter have the right to make out of the same lump of clay some pottery for noble purposes and some for common use?" (Romans 9:20-21).

If you, as a pastor, are able to get your leaders to take their eyes off other leaders and onto Christ, and if you will train them to be comfortable with the gifts that God has sovereignly given them, and if you will help them learn contentment in their circumstances, then you will have raised up men and women of God. And the world has still not seen what just one man or woman totally committed to Christ can do in the secular marketplace.

WARNING #2: DO NOT LOSE SIGHT OF THE ETERNAL

"Do you see all these great buildings?" replied Jesus. "Not one stone here will be left on another; every one will be thrown down. . . . Heaven and earth will pass away, but my words will never pass away" (Mark 13:2,31).

As Jesus continued His journey to the cross, He took time out to speak valuable truths to His disciples. Most of Mark 13 consists of His words to the three from the inner circle plus Andrew. Jesus wanted them to have an eternal mindset, to realize the importance of investing their time and resources on that which would last. As a pastor, you must equip your leaders in the very same way. Just as Jesus did, you must take their eyes off of buildings, organizations, and material gain and turn them to things that are eternal.

When I owned a large company and would occasionally be asked, "How is the business going?" I usually responded by reporting that sales were up or down or that profits had been good or poor. I talked about the latest new product or acquisition and sometimes worried out loud about a customer account that appeared to be in jeopardy. My constant challenge was to build the business, maintain the profit margin, and be financially stable. The institution demanded my constant attention.

A couple of years ago, I gave up the position of CEO. Three years earlier I had given up my interest in the business when I sold out after thirty-eight years of family ownership. The building we built some nineteen years before no longer bears our name, and one day the business will move to new and larger quarters. As the consolidation became reality, our individual business became a division, and then it was only a small part of a huge, national distribution firm. The institution that I had given most of my adult life for had gradually lost its identity.

Yes, the years of labor in the firm provided a comfortable income for my family and allowed us to do many things. It also gave me an opportunity to use my gifts and abilities to compete daily in our vast marketplace. I was able to travel to every part of the country and meet people from many walks of life. I was in one industry long enough to see some very small firms rise to tremendous success and also to see many long-term competitors, suppliers, and customers be broken by bankruptcy.

But when I (or anyone) get to the end of the road and look back, I must ask myself the questions "What is left?" and "What do I have that is not quickly destroyed by rust, removed by change, or lost by financial disaster?" The only things that remain are the people. They will endure the bankruptcies, the consolidations, and the change. People are the only things left from even the most successful business venture.

Many years ago, each of my brothers sold their interest in our firm during a seven-month period. My wife and I had a big decision to make. Should we also sell out and have someone else manage the firm, or hold on and try to take the firm to the next generation? After many weeks, we decided that God had placed us there for the people and that we would continue to invest in them. In making this choice, we faced a large financial exposure. Making a profit was still necessary, but that was just the entry ticket in order to continue to invest in people.

ETERNAL INVESTMENTS

Paul wrote in 1 Corinthians 3 that we can give our lives for "gold, silver, [and] costly stones" or for "wood, hay, or straw" (verse 12). In other words, we can give our lives for those things that will last for eternity or for those things that will soon perish. Using another metaphor, Jesus said that we can build our lives on a solid rock or build on a shaky foundation (see Matthew 7:24-26). He also warned us to labor, not for a reward that perishes but for the eternal (see John 6:27). Warn your leaders not to seek to build institutions, structures, buildings, or organizations at the neglect of the people right in front of them.

Over recent years, I have come to realize that business deals will come and go, but people last forever. Therefore, I have spent time with my staff members when they needed it. "Missy" was a young woman who had lost her parents at an early age. She would often come by my office, seeking encouragement. One day she explained that she needed to stay home in order to take care of her children. We lost a good worker, but I supported her in the hard choice she had to make.

"Kim," another employee, was also a young mother. We had to constantly limit her hours so that she could be with her husband and her child. I knew that I was responsible to God not for her work production but for her availability to her family.

"Gene" was a key executive living in another city. One day he showed up at my desk and began to identify with a near-death experience that I had had the summer before. Though we had worked together for years, finally the time was right to personally confront Gene with the gospel. I quietly shut the door and sat down across the table from him. After about thirty minutes of sharing, Gene prayed to receive Christ as his personal Savior. Ironically, I had been scheduled to be at an evangelistic luncheon that day, but it had been cancelled at the last minute. God had other plans for me that day. I got to pick fruit from a tree planted years before.

"Joe" was a young man who would often come in, close the door, and ask for my advice. Although we worked together every day and he was on my leadership team, he wanted extra time. We would talk about family, long-term career goals, finances, and spiritual matters. He appreciated my taking the time for him, and I was encouraged by his passion for God. Missy, Kim, Gene, and Joe are just four of the people that I have invested in over the years. They represent a solid portfolio.

Perhaps we need to constantly remind each other that although our assigned task is to build each of our institutions, our eternal mission is to build into the lives of people.

Your goal of equipping these workplace leaders has resulted in reproducing disciples of Jesus Christ in their natural spheres of influence. They will continually be involved in the process of evangelism and discipleship with many that they come in contact with. Your investment in their lives will reap benefits to many spiritual generations for years to come. These leaders are ready to leave your group and some will start new ones. Your relationship with them may change from that of mentor to peer, although you may continue to mentor them at various times in the future. As they go out to minister to others and train some, you will see the results of your ministry. You will be able to say along with John, "I have no greater joy than to hear that my children are walking in the truth" (3 John 1:4). These leaders are now your church's missionaries to a secular marketplace and Christ's representatives to a lost world.

ACTION STEPS

1. Share your own struggles in the area of comparison.

2. Discuss with each leader his or her personality type and spiritual gifts. If some are not sure what they are, now is the time to study these topics.

3. Ask each leader to list up to ten things that constantly demand his or her attention. Then ask each of them to divide that list of items into two columns: the temporal and the eternal.

4. Allow each leader to share one area that he or she needs to spend more time on and one area that needs to be limited or curtailed altogether.

5. Months or even years after these leaders leave your group, check on them. You have much invested in them, so have lunch together for mutual encouragement. The journey never ends!

YOU YOURSELVES
ARE OUR LETTER, WRITTEN
ON OUR HEARTS,
KNOWN AND READ BY
EVERYBODY.
YOU SHOW THAT YOU ARE A
LETTER FROM CHRIST,

THE RESULT OF OUR MINISTRY,
WRITTEN NOT WITH
INK BUT WITH THE SPIRIT
OF THE LIVING
GOD, NOT ON TABLETS
OF STONE BUT ON TABLETS
OF HUMAN HEARTS.

—2 CORINTHIANS 3:2-3

CHAPTER X

LEAVING A LEGACY

AS I WRITE this last chapter, my heart burns with a final message for you. Just last week, I received word that the consolidated corporation of which our former firm was a major division had filed for bankruptcy protection. The financial loss will be large, but the loss of dreams and of human capital will be much larger. Our family sold the firm nearly five years ago, but I continued as CEO for another three years. When I left, less than two years ago, our division was profitable and paying its bills on time, as it had done for nearly forty years. But several customer bankruptcies, unwise acquisitions, rapid growth, a poor economy, and unstable leadership contributed to the failure of the large national distribution firm.

TRANSITIONS IN LEADERSHIP

The company had been in our family for thirty-eight years prior to the sale. Our parents had mentored their three sons carefully. I had, in turn, mentored my son for six years (out of a ten-year plan). When he left to go into the ministry, we decided to sell the firm. No successor was in place. I told the new owners that I would stay for three to five years and train a successor to lead our division. The CEO of the large corporation was an excellent leader with similar experience to mine. However, for some reason, the investors thought that money and growth were more important than people, so they never replaced most of the original leaders that led the firms they acquired.

The acquisition vice president took my job with no formal training. He acquired three other firms, merged them into our division, and then left the firm eleven months after I did. Regardless of whose fault it was, without a succession plan in place, our division and ultimately a large national firm was headed for failure. My heart grieves for the employees, vendors, and customers that I had worked with for so many years. If I had stayed, could I have made a difference with just that one division? I believe that God led my son to leave for the ministry and led me to sell the firm, so that leaves many unanswered questions. One thing is certain: Leadership and transitions in leadership are far more important than most people think. This is true of a church, a business, or any organization.

YOUR SUCCESSOR IN THE KINGDOM OF GOD

This book has given you insights concerning the workplace leaders in your church and how you can better help them to minister in their spheres of influence. Hopefully, these relationships have been started and are developing. Now I want to speak with you about a special relationship.

Of all the leaders in your church, God will give you a special connection with one or two. I am not talking in this chapter about a successor for your church or one at your leaders' workplaces, although these principles will apply. Instead I refer to mentoring your successor in the kingdom of God. You will shepherd the flock of your church, and you will equip a group of young leaders, but you will only prepare a few to succeed you. These will be your legacy after you have left this world. Do you have a young pastor, a young businessperson, a seminary student, or another leader that you are preparing for a ministry that could be much larger and much different than yours? Are you investing for the future of the kingdom of God?

The goal is to transfer or pass on your vision to the next generation. Satan wants to cut off and deal a deathblow to the process. This is a spiritual battle.

TWELVE PRINCIPLES

Let me briefly share with you twelve biblical principles that may help you as you seek to transfer the vision to the next generation.

1. *Your Influence* — Your successors will receive respect because of your life and ministry. Joseph modeled this as he received a heritage from Abraham, Isaac, and Jacob (see Genesis 50:24; 2 Kings 13:23). Solomon received the blessings of God and others

because of his father, David (see 1 Kings 3:6; 5:1).

2. *Your Desire* — You want your successors to be successful; therefore, they should listen to your counsel. David gave specific instructions to his son, Solomon (see 1 Chronicles 22:5; 28:20). Jesus did the same for the disciples (see John 8:14).

3. *Your Perspective* — As a good leader you will look at:
   ◆ The long term, not the short term. (Jesus constantly had to get Peter's eyes off the temporal — see Matthew 17:4.)
   ◆ Their potential character, not their current one. (David prayed for Solomon — see 1 Chronicles 29:17-19; early in his association with Jesus, Peter thought of himself as a fisherman, but Jesus saw what he would become: a servant and an apostle. Peter eventually understood — see 2 Peter 1:1.)
   ◆ Their spirit, not their talent. (Moses saw this in his successor, Joshua — see Numbers 27:18.)
   ◆ Their humility in the process. (Peter went from a proud, independent spirit to a humbled man — see Luke 5:8; John 18:27.)

4. *Your Plan* — You must share your life with your successors. Jacob shared with his son Joseph (see Genesis 48:3). Jesus continually talked with the disciples (see Mark 7:17; 10:10). Paul had Timothy with him as he wrote 2 Corinthians, Philippians, Colossians, and 1–2 Thessalonians. Spend time with your successors, whether over lunch, at a ballgame, at a Christian conference, or at a business event.

5. *Your Principles* — Your successors will follow your principles, but not necessarily your methods, because methods change with each generation. Notice the attitude of Joshua (see Joshua 11:15). Solomon's problems occurred not because his methods were different but because he left the principles of God and turned his heart to other things (see 1 Kings 11:4). As my son and I worked together for six years, he brought in another generation with new methods, but the values were unchanged.

6. *Their Responsibility* — They are to learn from you.
   - They must get to know you well (Solomon — see 2 Chronicles 8:11).
   - They must remember your words (Jesus/Peter — see Mark 11:21).
   - They must listen carefully to your last words (David and Solomon — see 1 Chronicles 28:20).

7. *Their Goal* — They must stay on course and not neglect to honor you. Have you honored your mentors? Have you written and thanked them for their investment in you? Solomon got off course and paid a huge price (see 1 Kings 3:3; 11:4-6), but Elisha's commitment was total (see 19:21).

8. *Their Challenge* — You could "order" your people to follow the new, younger leader, but instead you must allow the leader to win over their hearts. Remember that leadership is not a position but a person. Your successors must verify the faith that you have in them. This takes time! David tried to order people to help his son, Solomon (see 1 Chronicles 22:17). Jesus chose instead to present the changed lives of Peter and John to the world (see Acts 4:13).

9. *Their Transformation* — As they mature as leaders, their weaknesses may become strengths. This is certainly true with Joshua and his courage (see Deuteronomy 31:7). For many years, I had a great weakness helping people one on one. Though this ability is not natural for me, I have learned to be adequate in this area because of the huge dividends it pays.

10. *Their Opportunity* — They will probably do more than you as a leader because of the foundation that you have laid. This was true with David and Solomon (see 1 Kings 1:37), Elisha (see 2 Kings 2:9), and the disciples (see John 14:12). My son has a ministry as a pastor today partly because of choices that his grandparents and parents made. Our daughters are women of God, nurtured by a long line of godly heritage. Hopefully, you will see your children (physically and spiritually) be able to build on the foundation of your life and ministry.

11. *Their Obstacle* — Watch out for family interference. The reverse side of all of these advantages is that we must train our children and disciples only to let them go. We then assume the position of counselor *when asked*. Do not ruin a good investment by interfering with their lives and ministries and what God wants to do uniquely through them. The Scriptures are full of wives, mothers, and others interfering in the lives of their children (see Genesis 21:10; 27:46; I Kings 1:13).

12. *Their Vision* — They must be careful to listen to God, not just you. Samuel modeled this (see I Samuel 3:9). He then shared the vision from God with his mentor, Eli (see 3:18).

ACTION STEPS

1. Pray that God would give you such a person.

2. Talk about "spiritual reproduction," "spiritual investments," and "legacy" in your sermons and teachings to create an environment of mentoring in your church.

3. Plan church activities that place younger people with those middle age and older. This, too, will foster a mentoring environment.

CONCLUSION

HAVE YOU EVER considered what Jesus would do if He were making decisions in the marketplace? That was the subject of a best-selling book first published in the late nineteenth century. *In His Steps,* by Charles Sheldon, tells the story of a group of community leaders asking the question "What would Jesus do?" as they went about their daily lives. We answer that question today by looking at the life of Jesus as it is portrayed in the Gospels.

Jesus spent time in the temple, but He spent most of His time in the marketplace, where He chose twelve men to be His disciples. He then let them watch and learn as He:

- *Told* everyone — the good news
- *Taught* many — to understand God's principles
- *Trained* some — to do the work of God
- *Equipped* a few — to reproduce followers
- *Modeled* a surrendered life — that they might catch the vision

These five activities answer the question "What would Jesus do?"

As a business executive I am untrained in your theological world, but I have pulled back the curtain and allowed you to get a good look at the marketplace. I pray that you have begun this sacrificial but worthwhile journey with some men and women from your church, forming your own groups of "twelve" and asking the ministry-changing question "How may I help you?"

I pray that you will aspire to be a tremendous equipper as well as a good evangelist, preacher, and teacher. Equippers overcome obstacles of organizations and tradition to raise up servant leaders who will transform their spheres of influence. You will mentor these leaders to not be detoured by failure or success and to learn the life of surrender.

And finally, you will release these leaders to minister creatively in their unique marketplaces and to model Christ in an increasingly secular culture. As these change agents focus on Christ instead of on themselves or others, they will give their lives to the eternal. You may have prepared many young leaders for the vocational ministry, but in equipping these marketplace leaders you may leave your greatest legacy.

Leaders in the marketplace who have been in your church regularly from Sunday to Sunday are asking, "What would Jesus do?" You can see "what Jesus did" as you reread the Gospels from the marketplace perspective. While you may have preached and taught for years and may even have mentored other young pastors, I have introduced you to the opportunity of transforming the marketplace in your community by equipping a few workplace leaders.

So I ask: What will you do? What living letters are you writing? What lasting investments are you making? If you have not already begun such a ministry, may God give you the vision and courage and strength to shepherd and release leaders to reach those whom you never could. I'll be praying for you.

SAMPLE MEETING TOPICS

MEETING 1

Topic: Software Copyrights

Scripture: 2 Samuel 21:1-14; Numbers 5:6-7

Case Study:

Jim had hired a consultant to design some analysis and reporting spreadsheets for a real estate limited partnership. When Jim and Norm began a home investment service company, the consultant modified those spreadsheets for the new business. Because he was relocating to another state, he left Jim and Norm with a copy of his commercial software that was used to generate the spreadsheets.

Almost a year later, while attempting to secure an operating manual, they discovered that they were in violation of the software copyright laws. The consultant had not received a license to copy the program used for the spreadsheet development and they were using copies of the original software.

Vaguely aware of the copyright laws, they were confused as to the appropriate way to respond to the situation.

Analysis

1. Define the problem/issue.
2. Identify the people involved.
3. Identify special circumstances and potential consequences.

Perspective (in light of every Christian business leader being a "priest" and every business a platform for ministry)

1. What actions should be taken?
2. How would God be honored?

Application

1. What insight have you gained concerning your own company?
2. What changes might you need to make in the operation of your position in the company?
3. What results would you hope to see?

MEETING 2

Topic: Borrowing Money

Scripture: Proverbs 12:15; 13:10; 14:12; 23:4-5; 27:12; Psalm 37:21

Case Study:

Two Christian businesspeople had an opportunity to buy an apartment building for slightly less than half of its $3 million appraised value. Their total down payment would be only $50,000 each, which they could easily afford, and a third party lender would provide a fixed rate mortgage at a reasonable interest rate.

The cash flow from the apartments, even at 60-percent occupancy, would be sufficient to cover all costs. The only requirement was that the borrowers both sign personally for the loan, in addition to securing the building as collateral.

"Analysis," "Perspective," and "Application" questions same as Meeting 1.

MEETING 3

Topic: Financial and Personnel Responsibility

Scripture: Proverbs 16:2-3; 2 Corinthians 9:8-11; James 5:13-15

Case Study:

A manufacturing company had developed its operating budget around the successful introduction and sales of a major product. When the product failed to sell at the rate projected, the company faced a serious financial crisis that threatened its stability.

The soundest response appeared to be to downsize the company to bring operating expenses in line with current sales. To do so would require the layoff of ten employees, many of whom were Christians. A deep dialogue ensued about the Christian-led company's responsibility to its employees and its responsibility to be a wise steward of its financial position and resources.

"Analysis," "Perspective," and "Application" questions same as Meeting 1.

MEETING 4

Topic: Restitution

Scriptures: Exodus 22:7-13; Luke 19:1-9; Matthew 5:23-24

Case Study:

Bill was a respected Christian leader and member of a visible evangelical church in his community. His influence and persuasive abilities were well known and appreciated. For more than twelve years, Bill's business had put together financial investments for professional people who were, for the most part, disinterested in the details of the investment process but who had excess capital to invest.

In his last four years of business, by his own personal confession, he was not successful in bringing one deal to completion. In each of those years, Bill collected a six-figure salary while his clients lost their entire investments. Bill was unable to fulfill promises he made, to a large degree because of mistakes he made personally and because of the incompetence of several staff members.

Bill was confronted by several clients and later by several Christian brothers regarding his responsibility for restitution. He angrily disagreed and refused further counsel.

"Analysis," "Perspective," and "Application" questions same as Meeting 1.

NOTE: The previous studies are used with the permission of Fellowship of Companies for Christ International. Workbooks of numerous case studies may be ordered from FCCI at 770-685-6000 or by e-mail at csr@fcci.org.

Using the following topics, plus others provided by your own group, you could use the previous format to tailor sessions to the needs of your particular leaders. The "Analysis," "Perspective," and "Application" questions are appropriate for any format. Simply ask your group for situations that they want to discuss. Then take those situations, add biblical references from your own study of the principles involved, and let the discussion flow!

Business Topics of Interest:

- Credit and collections
- Ownership with a nonChristian partner
- Taking a bribe
- Breach of contract
- Pricing procedures
- Honesty, surety
- Profitable relationships: business mergers and partnerships
- Compensation
- Management role models
- Decision-making responsibility
- Client relations
- Character
- Business practices
- Respect for government

- Employee wrongdoing
- Employee lifestyles
- Personal morality
- Promotion discrimination
- Unfair treatment

RESOURCES

BOOKS AND MAGAZINES

Beckett, John D. Loving Monday: Succeeding in Business Without Selling Your Soul. Downers Grove, Ill.: InterVarsity, 1998.

Blanchard, Ken and Michael O'Connor. Managing by Values. San Francisco: Bennett-Kochler Publishing, 1997.

Boa, Kenneth and Gail Burnett. Wisdom at Work: A Biblical Approach to the Workplace. Colorado Springs, Colo.: NavPress, 2000.

Burkett, Larry. Business by the Book: A Complete Guide of Biblical Principles for the Workplace. Nashville: Nelson, 1998.

Crane, Christopher and Mike Hamel. Executive Influence: Impacting Your Workplace for Christ. Colorado Springs, Colo.: NavPress, 2003.

DePree, Max. Leadership Is an Art. New York: Doubleday, 1989.

Guiness, Os. The Call: Finding and Fulfilling the Central Purpose of Your Life. Nashville: Word, 1998.

Hammond, Pete, R. Paul Stevens, and Todd Svanol. The Marketplace Annotated Bibliography. Downers Grove, Ill.: InterVarsity, 2002. (A Christian guide to 1,200 books on work, business, and vocation)

Humphreys, Kent and Davidene. Show and Then Tell: Presenting the Gospel Through Daily Encounters. Chicago: Moody, 2000.

Lawrence, William D. and Jack A. Turpin. Beyond the Bottom Line: Where Faith and Business Meet. Chicago: Moody, 1994.

Marr, Steve. Business Proverbs: Daily Wisdom for the Workplace. Grand Rapids, Mich.: Revell/Baker, 2001. Also contact www. businessproverbs.com (250 devotionals).

Marshall, Rich. God at Work: Discovering the Anointing for Business. Shippensburg, Pa.: Destiny Image, 2000.

Noah, Laura L. Believers in Business. Nashville: Nelson, 1994.

Pascarella, Perry. Christ-Centered Leadership: Thriving in Business by Putting God in Charge. Rocklin, Calif.: Prima Publishing, 1999.

Pollard, C. William. The Soul of the Firm. Grand Rapids, Mich.: Zondervan/Harper Business, 1996.

The Work in Life Study Bible. Nashville: Nelson, 1996.

RECOMMENDED WORKPLACE MINISTRIES

FELLOWSHIP OF COMPANIES FOR CHRIST INTERNATIONAL (FCCI)

"...transforming the world through Christ, one company leader at a time..."

4201 NORTH PEACHTREE ROAD
SUITE 200
ATLANTA, GA 30431
770-685-6000

WWW.FCCI.ORG

In pursuit of Christ's eternal objectives, FCCI equips and encourages business leaders to operate their businesses and conduct their personal lives in accordance with biblical principles.

Members believe that as their influence grows, their lives become an example for others to follow and Christ is honored in the workplace.

FCCI is also known as the brand Christ@Work in the U.S. and Crown Companies, internationally.

Kent Humphreys served as President of FCCI from 2002 to 2007. Since 2008, Kent has served as FCCI's International Ambassador – traveling, speaking, writing, and mentoring.

Breakthrough Business Leadership (BBL)

877-CEO-2CEO

www.bblforum.com

BBL Forum (BBL) is a member-based organization comprised of qualified Christian CEOs, business owners and company presidents. In short, those who run businesses and those who would benefit from the knowledge and expertise of professionals who are like-minded both spiritually and corporately.

Business as Mission Network

www.businessasmissionnetwork.com

A resource with news, resources, and tools to turn good business into great ministry.

C-12 Group

336-841-7100

www.c12group.com

C12 hopes to serve to those the Lord has already called to lead their life, including their businesses, for His purposes. As a Christian leadership development organization, C12 helps teach other to best use their position as CEO, Owner or President to share the joy of serving Christ daily.

CBMC (USA)

800-566-2262

www.cbmc.com

One hundred thousand people in more than seventy countries participate in CBMC (formerly the Christian Business Men's Committee, now Connecting Business and the Marketplace to Christ), an organization that ministers to all levels of businesspeople through events such as luncheons and small-group Bible studies.

CBMC INTERNATIONAL

402-431-0002

www.cbmcint.org

Beginning with a small group of business and professional leaders in Chicago, CBMC International has grown to an active global ministry with Christian business associations on six continents in more than 80 countries. CBMC International serves and supports those national ministries by equipping and engaging key leaders within the organization.

CHRISTIAN BUSINESS DAILY

941-377-9384

www.christianbusinessdaily.com

A resource for any Christian entrepreneur or business owner who needs resources, tools, and training. The organizatio works to provide the HOW to running a Kingdom-minded business.

CORPORATE CHAPLAINS OF AMERICA

919-570-0700

www.iamchap.org

CCA provides genuine "caring in the workplace" through its workforce of Certified Workplace Chaplains. The mission of CCA's chaplains is to build relationships with employees with the hope of gaining permission to share the good news of Jesus Christ with them in a nonthreatening manner.

CROWN FINANCIAL MINISTRIES

800-722-1976

www.crown.org

Crown's mission is to equip people worldwide to learn, apply, and teach God's financial principles so they may know Christ more intimately, be free to serve Him, and help fund the Great Commission.

DISCERNING THE TIMES

707-578-7700

www.discerningthetimes.com

This website is designed to stimulate a fresh discussion on the underlying presuppositions and ethics which will affect the future of individuals, families, communities and nations. The site includes current events analysis, public policy debates, audio, and video posts. It is a useful tool in bridging the gap between those already seeing the Kingdom and others who are seeking answers for the future of our world.

HENRY BLACKABY MINISTRIES

770-603-2900

www.blackaby.org

Henry Blackaby holds regular conference calls with Christian CEOs across the country. He focuses on helping men and women at work.

HIS CHURCH AT WORK

404-935-5757

www.hischurchatwork.org

Their mission is to exhort the local church to join God where He is working in the workplace and to assist pastors and local churches in helping men and women understand, experience, and fulfill their God-given calling of work as ministry.

INTEGRITY RESOURCE CENTER

913-782-9333

www.integritymoments.com

This organization is dedicated to changing the workplace for Christ by providing biblically-based resources, training, and counsel to business and ministry leaders.

INTERNATIONAL CHRISTIAN CHAMBER OF COMMERCE

562-597-4475

www.iccc.net

Aiding in the networking and mobilizing of Kingdom entrepreneurs, executives, educational and governmental leaders into the purposeful, strategic, global Kingdom initiatives underway in our day.

INTERNATIONAL COALITION OF
WORKPLACE MINISTRIES

678-455-6262 x103

www.icwm.net

A fellowship of workplace believers who want to ignite leaders for workplace transformation by modeling Jesus Christ. They do this by inspiring, connecting and equipping leaders who want to transform the workplace for Christ. The ICWM website is a clearinghouse for information, resources and organizations in the faith and work movement.

MADE TO MATTER

978-626-1097

www.madetomatter.org

Madetomatter.org was founded in 2007 as the flagship site and public face of Desired Haven Ministries, Inc. The chief aim of Desired Haven Ministries is to help people get to a place where they're able to recognize and consider the great love of God.

Marketplace Chaplains USA

972-385-7657

www.mchapusa.com

Begun in 1984, a faith-based Employee Assistance Program that provides a chaplain service to secular businesses. These chaplains care for employees and their families, partnering with client companies in locations across the United States.

Marketplace Leaders

678-455-6262

www.marketplaceleaders.org

Exists to help men and women discover and fulfill God's unique and complete purposes through their workplace calling. They do this through the TGIF Daily Devotional and other books authored by Os Hillman, live speaking opportunities, marketplace mentoring, consulting and partnering services for businesses and ministries, tools for local churches, and many more equipping resources and services found at their online Christian Workplace bookstore and throughout their website.

Ministry in Daily Life

608-274-4823

www.ivmdl.org

InterVarsity Christian Fellowship/USA is committed to Discipleship of the Mind (learning and thoughtful Biblical reflection in every area of life) and Whole Life Stewardship (proclaiming Jesus as Lord over all creation and culture and integrating faith, life and vocation in service to Him). To this end, Marketplace Ministries and Ministry in Daily Life (www.ivmdl.org) were developed by Pete Hammond in the 1980s to provide resources, networks and encouragement to those pursuing these values.

Priority Associates

919-954-1600

www.priorityassociates.org

Priority Associates is a network of creative and corporate professionals, seeking to balance our professional, personal and spiritual lives. Active now in over twenty cities across the country, Priority Associates is a resource for young professionals, providing opportunities to explore issues of success, personal leadership and significance in a variety of venues.

Selling Among Wolves Sales Seminar

941-377-9384

www.sellingamongwolves.net

Selling Among Wolves is a Christian-based sales seminar taught by Michael Pink. It is an excellent teaching workshop, helping Christians apply biblical sales concepts.

Strategic Christian Services

707-578-7700

www.gostrategic.org

Seek to help people by equipping them and those they influence by providing to them an effective strategy to do so. They educate, train, and work with people who have a heart to help bring God's transformation to a fallen world.

Wise Counsel

904-332-0425

www.wisecounselonline.com

This site is primarily designed for business executives who want to know more on how biblical principles are working in their life as well as those who are open to hear opinions from other men and women on how to improve and become more compatible with their calling and purpose in leading their business.

NOTES

CHAPTER 1

1. Os Hillman, Today God Is First (Shippensburg, Pa.: Destiny Image, 2000), p. 358.

CHAPTER 3

1. "It's Not a Program or a Tool. It's About People," Leadership Network.Net Fax, no. 121 (April 12, 1999).

2. Wayne Cordeiro, quoted in "Doing Church As a Team," Leadership Network Explorer, no. 30 (February 12, 2001).

3. Glenn Wagner, Escape from Church, Inc. (Grand Rapids, Mich.: Zondervan, 1999), p. 142.

CHAPTER 4

1. Philip B. Gove, ed., Webster's Seventh New Collegiate Dictionary (Springfield, Mass.: G. & C. Merriam Company, 1963).

2. Richard Halverson, "Perspective" devotional letter, Vol. XLV, No. 11, December 1, 1993.

3. Marva J. Dawn, "How Christian Worship Forms a Missional Community," Modern Reformation, May/June 2000, p. 28.

4. Peter Senge, as quoted by Len Sweet in, "Eight Catch 22's of the 21st Century," Leadership Network Explorer, no. 12 (June 5, 2000), p. 5.

5. Jim Craddock, Scope Ministries Report, July 1999.

6. Leith Anderson, Leadership That Works (Minneapolis: Bethany, 1999), p. 75.

7. Sweet, p. 7.

8. Leroy Armstrong, as quoted by Sweet, p. 7.

9. Margaret Wheatley, as quoted by Sweet, p. 7.

10. Sweet, p. 6.

11. Peter Senge, as quoted by Sweet, p. 5.

12. Ken Blanchard, as quoted by Sweet, p. 5.

CHAPTER 5

1. Ford Madison. Used by permission.

2. Larry Burkett. Used by permission.

3. Anthony Campolo. Used by permission.

4. Patrick Morley. Used by permission.

CHAPTER 6

1. Kent and Davidene Humphreys, Show and Then Tell: Presenting the Gospel Through Daily Encounters (Chicago: Moody, 2000), pp. 143-153.

2. Lorne Sanny. Used by permission.

CHAPTER 7

1. Richard Halverson, "Perspective" devotional letter, vol. XVIV, no. 21 (October 7, 1992.)

CHAPTER 9

1. Michael Gott. Used by permission.

ABOUT THE AUTHOR

KENT HUMPHREYS has been a leader in the marketplace for nearly forty years. While owning and operating a nationwide general merchandise distribution firm, he worked with the nation's largest retailers. After selling the family business in 1997, Kent continued to be involved in real estate, manufacturing, and medical distribution businesses. From 2002 through 2007, he was president of Fellowship of Companies for Christ International (also know as Christ@Work), an organization that equips and encourages Christian business owners, executives, and professionals who desire to use their companies as platforms for ministry. During Kent's tenure, the ministry expanded from three nations to putting small groups of business leaders into more than twenty nations.

For many years, Kent has spent much of his time ministering to business leaders and pastors across the country through speaking, writing, and mentoring. He has spoken in more than twenty different seminaries in the U.S. and overseas. He has served on the board of The Navigators, key seminaries, and local hospitals.

Kent and his wife of 42 years, Davidene, have three children and eight grandchildren, and reside in Oklahoma City. They have authored several books together including *Show and then Tell: Presenting the Gospel through Daily Encounters* (Moody) and *Shepherding Horses: Understanding God's Plan for Transforming Leaders.*

Kent Humphreys
PO Box 271054
Oklahoma City, OK 73137-1054
Phone: 405-949-0070 x102 or 405-917-1681 x102
Email: kent@fcci.org or khumphreys@ahpartners.com
Website: www.lifestyleimpact.com

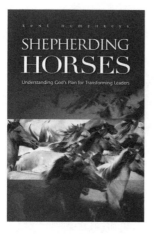

Shepherding Horses (Volume I)
Understanding God's Plan for
Transforming Leaders
(Diakota Publishing)

Kent's most well-received book yet! This
50-page guide to Understanding God's Plan for
Transforming Leaders is a must-read for any
pastor and the strong and driven business
leaders (horses) that he shepherds. Kent looks
at a biblical view of "horses" and shares with
pastors an effective way to partner with these
business leaders – building bridges of
acceptance and understanding.

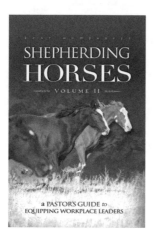

Shepherding Horses (Volume II)
A Pastor's Guide for Equipping
Workplace Leaders
(Diakota Publishing)

In this book, Kent encourages pastors to invest
in the incredible resource they have – the
business leaders in their churches. The book is
full of practical and possible ideas for
shepherding, encouraging and releasing these
leaders for ministry in the place they
understand best - their business world.

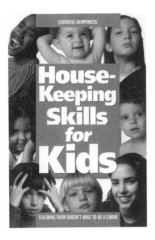

Housekeeping Skills for Kids
Teaching Them Doesn't Have to Be a Chore

Davidene's book, Housekeeping Skills for Kids: Teaching Them Doesn't Have to be a Chore" has proven to be a best-seller. In it she provides simple and practical steps for parents of any-aged children to train them in skills that they will need to create and run their own home someday. Full of stories, encouragement, and ideas, this book is an inspiration to any parent trying to develop their kids' domestic skills. It covers everything from cooking, to organization, to use of tools, to planning great parties.

Encouragement for Your Journey Alone
Meditations of Hope for Widows
(Tate Publishing

This wonderful little book is a gift of hope and encouragement for widows. It is a compilation of meditations, which the author suggests reading at the pace of one per week. This gives thinking and praying time over each meditation. Kent Humphreys has written a letter each month for nine years to many widows; this book has been birthed from that long-standing ministry and is a special gift to women who have a special place in God's heart.

Between the Phone Call and the Funeral
(Tate Publishing)

Have you ever wondered what to do for a grieving family? Do you find yourself taking food to the house, feeling a bit nervous about what to say? Do you end your visit by saying something like, "If you need anything, call me"? You mean it, but you are not sure what would be helpful. This book is your answer. It is the best gift you could give, and the ideas in it are the best things you could do for these hurting friends. Buy one now, and have it before you need it, because you will need it. Buy another one to put in your church's office for the next church family who needs it. Helping those who grieve is a wonderful ministry, one which blesses the giver as much as the receiver.

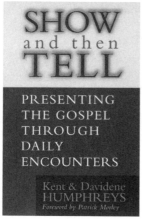

Show and then Tell
Presenting the Gospel Through Daily Encounters

(Moody Publishing)

How can we become confident in sharing our faith, both in action and word? How do we make ourselves available to others, Christian and non-Christian, to share what God has done in our own lives? How do we encourage them to trust God more? In Show and then Tell, Kent and Davidene encourage Christians that God has called every one of us to evangelism. He has given us unique personalities and gifts to reach our world for Christ. Our lives have extraordinary possibilities when we call on Jesus to give us the strength to share our faith – naturally.

COMING SOON!!!

Christ@Work – Opening Doors
Impacting Your Workplace for Jesus Christ

(Diakotia Publishing)

Kent shares how you can impact your co-workers, vendors, customers, and even your competitors for Jesus Christ in your workplace. He shows you what to do, how to do it, and when to start. He shares the steps to walking through open doors in the workplace that God will undoubtedly provide for you.

Find these books and more at
Lifestyle Impact Ministries

PO Box 271054
Oklahoma City, OK 73107
405-949-0070 x101

www.lifestyleimpact.com

LIM is the resource ministry of Kent Humphreys and his wife, Davidene. Access our website for free downloads of ministry letters and handouts, PowerPoint presentations from various speaking engagements, audio recordings and more.

"Many Christians embrace the salt and the light metaphor Jesus used in His Sermon on the Mount with only a vague grasp on its meaning of strong penetration. Salt purifies, refreshes, and flavors; light dispels darkness. Both are vigorous agents of change, but how does it really work in the day-to-day world?

With plentiful real-life evidence, Show and then Tell takes the reader like a hidden camera along with its two wide-awake and deeply caring authors to see the simplicity of our Lord's formula for living. Here is a book crafted for every believer in Jesus Christ – an intriguingly readable and profitable short course in making a difference wherever, whenever and however the circumstances."

HOWARD G. HENDRICKS
Distinguished Professor
Chairman, Center for Christian
Leadership, Dallas Theological Seminary

"Kent Humphreys knows the marketplace, and his wife Davidene knows the homefront...and their passion is to make Christ so unmistakably clear and believable that He would be unavoidable to everyone they meet. Show and then Tell shows us how."

CLIFF BARROWS

"This book is not theory. Kent and Davidene Humphreys live what they teach. Their lives have the aroma of the "smoke of the battle". They are intensely engaged and practically living the life of Christ in the marketplace and neighborhood. This is a "must read" for everyone who wants to impact their world for Christ."

JERRY E. WHITE, PH.D.
Chairman, The Navigators